GOOD WORK, GRIT & GRATITUDE

The Bittersweet Lessons of the Lemonade Generation

A Memoir

Illustration of the family by Emily Koffsky.

Cover and page design by Anna Myers Sabatini.

Library of Congress Control Number: 2023919375
ISBN: 979-8-9858064-8-9
Ebook ISBN: 979-8-9858064-9-6

Green Fire Press
PO Box 377 Housatonic MA 01236

Publisher's Cataloging-in-Publication data

Names: Dubow, Adrian, author. | Koffsky, Laura, author. Title: Good work, grit & gratitude : the bittersweet lessons of the lemonade generation, a memoir / Adrian Dubow & Laura Koffsky. Description: Housatonic, MA: Green Fire Press, 2023. Identifiers: LCCN: 2023919375 | ISBN: 979-8-9858064-8-9 (paperback) | 979-8-9858064-9-6 (ebook) Subjects: LCSH Dubow, Adrian. | Koffsky, Laura. | Philanthropists—Biography. | Community Organizations. | Adult children living with parents. | COVID-19 Pandemic, 2020- | Parent and adult child. | Adult children—Family relationships. | BISAC BIOGRAPHY & AUTOBIOGRAPHY / Personal Memoirs | BIOGRAPHY & AUTOBIOGRAPHY / Women | FAMILY & RELATIONSHIPS / Parenting / Parent & Adult Child | BIOGRAPHY & AUTOBIOGRAPHY / Business | Classification: LCC HQ755.86 .D83 2023 | DDC 306.874—dc23

GOOD WORK, GRIT & GRATITUDE

The Bittersweet Lessons of
the Lemonade Generation

A Memoir

ADRIAN DUBOW & LAURA KOFFSKY

Green
Fire
Press

Housatonic
Massachusetts

Jacob Steph Emily Louie Dan Andrew Laura Adrian Brian Ken Rachel

Illustration by Emily Koffsky

To our parents, grandparents, and those who are no longer
with us, for their love, tenacity, and wisdom. To our
husbands and children, our Quarenteams in the Lemonade
Generation, for their humor, candor, unconditional love, and
encouragement, and for allowing us to share their stories.

To the future—our children, grandchildren,
professionals, and leaders in our communities.
May we all continue to work together to lift each
other up and embrace life's bittersweet moments.

GOOD WORK, GRIT & GRATITUDE

The Bittersweet Lessons of the Lemonade Generation

A Memoir

ADRIAN DUBOW & LAURA KOFFSKY

Contents

Preface

September 2023

United States Surgeon General Dr. Vivek Murthy and a panel of six other surgeons general met in September 2023 to discuss the public mental crisis of loneliness, isolation, and lack of connection in our country. According to Murthy, "Our disconnection from one another is one of the most important foundational issues we are dealing with in society today."

It had been more than three years since the first news of some strange virus that was making its way across the ocean—three years since words such as lockdown, mask, vaccine, PPO, PPE, rapid test, and remote work became familiar parts of the everyday vernacular. And here we are, still grappling with the effects of our post-COVID-19 world.

The coronavirus shifted the world into survival mode, forcing people to forge ahead in both their personal and professional lives despite myriad challenges and setbacks. What did we do while hoarding groceries and obsessively watching Dr. Anthony Fauci and Dr. Deborah Birx, wondering which scarf she would be sporting that day? We decided to write a book.

The pandemic was the lens that helped us clarify what matters most in our lives. While the uncertainty in our world brought struggle and sadness, it also revealed some of the best and most generous sides of humanity. For some, there have been personal losses; for others, unexpected growth; and for most, recalibration. Each of us has been confronted with the daily issues in our world. The pandemic taught us to stay open-minded, and optimistic in the face of stress and suffering. As our world continues to evolve, the lesson of turning lemons into lemonade will always be relevant. Often it is in life's bitterest moments that we find the good and appreciate the sweetness.

Writing a book is a challenging, illuminating, often frustrating, and deeply rewarding process. With either unabashed bravery or complete naïveté, we have put our full hearts into chronicling our pandemic experiences. What began as a project to add structure and purpose to what felt like very unstructured, purposeless days morphed over time into this memoir that contained our honest and humorous observations. It became a commentary on our changing world and a reality check of our relationships with our adult children and colleagues. It is a time capsule that we hope captures the profundity of the moment. The seeds for this book were sown by countless conversations with colleagues, family, and friends, each of them teaching us something important about this unique time and the synergies that exist across the generations.

Everyone has a unique story to tell about their individual journey while the world was on pause. We are sharing ours, recognizing and acknowledging our privilege in having had the time and resources to work on this book. We are also grateful for the gift of our twenty-seven years of friendship that offered us the opportunity to work on it together. While others were virtually schooling students at the kitchen table, we lived with our adult children and cared for our aging parents. We saw our professional lives in the nonprofit world change almost overnight and watched as our colleagues adapted to a remote world where the term *home office* acquired a new meaning.

This time of flux propelled us to dig deeper and ultimately do better, changing the way we work, live, and think. As painful as the days in lockdown were, they were also a time of personal development and empowerment. They helped us harness our energy and clarify our core values. Our sons, Brian and Andrew were both 26 at the time. They harnessed their energies to the extreme and decided to train for an Ironman triathlon. The memory of sitting on the sidelines, watching the months of training necessary to complete this athletic endeavor, still has us in a cold sweat.

In contrast, as women in our fifties, we watched while our lives slowed nearly to a grinding halt. With no training manual, we did our best to keep pace with the hurdles the pandemic continued to create. Ultimately, our sons' Ironman became somewhat of a metaphor of our own triumph, and each of us emerged more confident, more resilient, and with a greater understanding of each other's journey.

We are grateful for the insights both of us gained, and now we're focused on stepping to the sideline while remaining steadfast in our commitment to make the world a better place for our children's generation and future generations. The passing of the baton to the rising leaders of tomorrow is thoughtful and intentional good work. Together we can appreciate each other's differences and find solutions to the challenges that lie ahead. Our hope is that this book will serve as a catalyst to spark future dialogue so we can inspire the next generation of dynamic leaders to continue to do the important work needed to strengthen communities.

We have marveled at the growth we've seen in our adult children and in ourselves. We have a new appreciation for what is to be learned from future generations and the potential collaborative energy that can galvanize our communities. Learning to find the good, the sweetness, and the joy—even during the sourest of times—is the ethos of the Lemonade Generation.

—Adrian Dubow and Laura Koffsky
Miami, Florida

Introduction

Mask Up and Shut Up

With the onset of COVID-19, people across different generations found themselves unexpectedly navigating days, weeks, and months of living under the same roof where every day felt like *Groundhog Day.* We watched our adult children march back into our homes for what we thought was a short visit and then quickly realized there was no departure in sight. Like many, our kids readjusted to adult life, now living in their childhood bedrooms while we grew reaccustomed to living with them, their pets, and their dirty laundry.

We had raised our children to be smart and independent—and suddenly we had a hard time relating to our smart and independent children. Ironically, during a time when we literally wore masks on our faces, some of the most transparent, honest, unscripted, and humorous family conversations took place, giving us the ability to see each other under a different lens—as adults. Our roles, once familiar, became redefined. We were suddenly staring into our own sitcom—*Mask Up and Shut Up*—an original drama and reality TV show like no other.

Our Story

We are two dear friends, once professionals working in the retail and advertising industries. We met when our sons—Adrian's son Brian and Laura's son Andrew—were in preschool together. Having spent more than two decades as full-time mothers and community leaders, we leveraged our skill sets and launched a business—Good Work Miami, LLC. We found ways to help connect people to the good work done by nonprofit organizations in our community and beyond. We derive purpose by making a positive impact where we can and in helping serve the missions of charitable organizations.

When the pandemic began and the world paused, we were more grateful than ever for our partnership and this project. Our twice-weekly Zoom "therapy" writing sessions kept us forward-thinking and gave structure to our lives. It was a reason to talk to people and to keep talking to each other, processing the enormity of what was happening in the world and to us as women who were now getting "oldish." We realized that maybe it wasn't all about us anymore.

We could never have anticipated that a global pandemic would derail the world, much less provide a detour that would suddenly reroute us back into full-time parenting roles—again. Although we have more than fifty years of combined parenting wisdom, we're not experts. We're just moms who have truly loved raising our kids and have always felt a great sense of purpose and responsibility to teach our children to make a positive impact. When we saw our young adult children—two for Adrian and three for Laura—return home in March 2020 with backpacks in hand for what we thought was a short-term visit, we began to shift professional gears. With an abundance of caution and an unnerving amount of hygiene, we later decided to share our stories about this very unique time in our lives.

COVID-19 was the great disrupter that somehow gave us clarity and creativity. We landed front-row seats to witness how our children operate as adults. We learned that they know a lot about a lot of things that we do not. We felt their deep care for others and for the world, and we conversed with them honestly and inquisitively like never before. When our children last lived in our homes, we'd been their parents, their teachers, their mentors, their cheerleaders, and their emotional supporters. This unexpected experience of Baby Boomers and Millennials living and working together led to the creation of an experiment we humorously refer to as the BooMillennial Lab.

We have also reflected on all we can learn from the generations that came before us. Our parents and grandparents learned to make lemonade when life handed them lemons. Will our children be able to do the same? Previous generations stayed the course and remained in jobs for years, even decades. By contrast, today's Generation Z (those after Millennials) has come of age during the pandemic, sitting in sweatpants and staring at their computer screens. Now, as the world seeks to step into a new version of normal, Gen Z is questioning their commitment to in-office work, seeking flexibility in their workday, a sustainable work-life balance, and benefits such as comprehensive healthcare coverage and mental health support.

Every generation faces challenges, but aside from COVID-19, it seems that today's Millennials and Gen Z have experienced more than their share of hardships. That list includes war and violence, mass shootings, climate change, challenges to women's reproductive rights, anti-Semitism, white supremacy, polarized political divide, widening wealth disparity, technology, social media, artificial intelligence, and the constant pressure and immediacy of information overload.

The problems that past generations helped create are now sitting squarely on the shoulders of our children in whom we have invested so much time, emotion, and financial resources. Somehow it all seems too much for us problem-solving, over-indulging, self-involved control freaks to fix. So what do Baby Boomers who thought we had all the answers do now?

The evolution of the Lemonade Generation has been extraordinary, and the journey has only just begun. On a personal level, we have gained a great appreciation for this new generation of brave, smart, resourceful people. We have finally been able to see our children as owners of their own lives, and we are grateful to just be along for the ride, this time from the passenger's seat. It's about time, because we're exhausted!

May we never experience a time like this again, but may we never forget this time.

1

Generation to Generation

Live Your Legacy but
Lose the Luggage

March 2020

Adrian

Visitation was not allowed. My eighty-six-year-old mother, JoAnn, darted out of her apartment building, her mask covering her fully made-up face. Blue dishwashing gloves on her hands, she pushed her cart to retrieve the groceries and other essential items I had in my car and was bringing to her on a sweltering Monday afternoon. Since she was locked down, or "in prison" as she often said with a chuckle, I met Mom on grocery days and had twelve to fifteen minutes to see each other in person and chat as we sat on benches that were eight feet apart.

On this day, my mom walked toward me with a faster stride than usual, indicating that she had something important to tell me. She had just finished watching a program on the "resident channel" in her apartment about the history of the Spanish flu in 1918. She had taken diligent notes and gave me a detailed recap of the program. It was meaningful, not only because we were currently living through a global pandemic but also because her mother—my grandmother Rebecca—lost her mother to the Spanish flu in 1918.

Grandma Rebecca always cried when she spoke about her mother, which was not very often. She and her four sisters grew up in Atchison, Kansas, at the turn of the twentieth century. They lived a privileged life, their father making a good living in the scrap metal business. Both my grandmother and her mother fell ill to the Spanish flu early on during that pandemic. My grandmother survived, but her mother, who was in the next bedroom, died.

This strain of the Spanish flu first appeared in the United States in Fort Riley, Kansas. It was transported there by military men returning home from Europe and then made its way through Topeka and into Atchison. It wasn't until I lived through the COVID-19 pandemic that I had a small idea of what my grandmother had endured so many years ago when her mother died. Why didn't I ask her more questions? Why didn't she and her sisters share more about that unprecedented time in their lives? Five sisters lost their mother in 1918 to a tragic virus, and they rarely spoke about it.

I am saddened by the magnitude of my grandma's grief while she became a pseudo-mother to her younger sisters. Her responsibilities and emotional pain must have been huge, yet she always held her head high, charged forward with optimism, and had a strong faith. In my grandmother's ninety-seven years, she endured a pandemic that claimed her mother, two depressions, two World Wars, and the usual ups and downs of life. Living through each challenge gave her the uncanny ability to adapt to a new normal.

My Grandmother Rebecca was a member of the Lost Generation—those who came of age during World War I and often found themselves directionless survivors in the early postwar period. They tended to suppress their emotions and never shared their "dirty laundry." Grandma raised six children, four of whom were part of the Greatest Generation born between 1921 and 1927. They became adults during the Great Depression and watched their parents lose their business, money, and hope. Her other two children, which included my mother, were part of the Silent Generation—one that, according to U.S. Census data, was smaller than preceding generations because the Great Depression and World War II resulted in fewer childbirths.

My mother inherited her strong work ethic from her parents and older siblings who believed in the value of hard work and perseverance. Incredibly resourceful, they did what they had to do to survive. They didn't have the luxury of asking themselves if they were happy or fulfilled in their jobs. They were just grateful to be employed and happy to wear hand-me-down clothing. They believed that with integrity, kindness, faith, and love, good would prevail.

When the COVID-19 pandemic began, the independent living facility where my mother lived went on lockdown. Every day around noon, I called to ask how she was doing, although I was sure nothing had changed since yesterday and not much would by tomorrow. My mother ate breakfast, washed the dishes, and read the paper—usually on her terrace. On those midday phone calls, we talked about how she planned to spend the rest of her day. Later, she headed downstairs for the dinner served by the facility, and she ate it alone. Weather permitting, she sat outside with a few friends for a quick chat before heading back to her apartment by 7:00 p.m. for another evening in isolation. But Mom never said she was lonely or bored. She always had an optimistic attitude.

A few weeks after the COVID lockdown, Mom heard some of us talking about the Zoom calls we were having for both work and social connections. She wanted to get in on the action. Her outdated computer wasn't equipped for Zoom calls, so in my mother's usual style—always determined to join the party—she called Dell, made friends with the customer support representative, and purchased the proper equipment to bring her old computer into the Zoom era. Within a few weeks, the accessories arrived and were installed. She joined us in the Zoom room, reconnecting at a time of difficult disconnection.

We can learn a lot from the generations before us—how they survived and thrived under the toughest conditions. Their wise words were often said in our households—"This, too, shall pass" and "One day at a time." These philosophies have kept our families and country afloat even in our darkest days.

In contrast, the narrative of the Baby Boomer generation is not so optimistic. It was the largest American generation, born between 1946 and 1964 when higher education was more obtainable, opportunity and independence were promoted, and sex, drugs, and rock and roll made their debut. The job market was strong, and suburban living expanded. Shopping malls were magnified, along with everything else—from large station wagons to platform shoes and long hair for both men and women. It was also a time of agitation for racial equity and women's rights, as well as the assassination of a president and the horrors of the Vietnam War, which sparked protests and political disarray. Boomers have lived large, had a good time, taken a lot from the planet, and are now watching their children wrestle with the consequences.

I grew up in Leawood, Kansas, a suburb of Kansas City, in a fantastic and wholesome Midwestern community. Although I have lived in Miami for almost forty years, I still like to refer to myself as "simple Midwestern folk." Both of my parents worked very hard to give my brother and me opportunities they had not had. My father and his mother immigrated from the part of Russia now known as Ukraine. He was thirteen years old. Sponsored by an uncle who had immigrated a few years earlier and a national nonprofit agency, they were resettled in Kansas City, Missouri.

Can you imagine fleeing a communist country and ending up smack dab in middle America where you can't speak a word of English? Dad was placed in kindergarten to learn English. He quickly moved through elementary school until he was ready for his age-appropriate grade. He graduated with honors from both high school and college and then proceeded to work hard—really hard. I vividly remember my father as a traveling salesman, returning home usually on Thursday afternoons from his weekly journeys. I would run out of the house with open arms to greet him, often falling and skinning my knees on the gravel driveway. My mother applied mercurochrome, Band-Aids, and kisses, a routine that would likely take place the following week. Silly me.

My mother is an innate optimist, a consummate professional, and a lover of love, family, and humor. She has an inspiring ability to love deeply and laugh often. These are truly her favorite things, especially at this point in her life. My childhood was filled with lots of laughter, love, and faith. Lucky me. But there was also divorce, death, and many skinned knees. They all contributed to my strength, empathy, gratitude, and humor—what I came to call my Band-Aids for a skinned heart.

At a young age I learned that life is not perfect and that everyone has some semblance of functionally dysfunctional baggage in their trunk. But my Midwestern foundation established my core values, for which I am forever grateful. Although I traded barbeques and sunflowers for stone crabs and palm trees, my husband, Kenny, and I raised our children with the same basic values we were raised with. Treat people how you want to be treated. Work hard. Help wherever you can, and move through the world with kindness and appreciation.

I was a professional woman who became a professional parent. I was goal-oriented and organized, and I thought it was my job to instill in my children these values while also catering to their every need and want. No one demanded this of me; it was just what I did. I was always thrilled when my kids included me in their plans, especially in their teenage years. I thought they needed me, which they did. But at the same time, I needed them. They gave me an incredible sense of fulfillment and joy.

When our first child, Rachel, came into the world, she had a cry like a little lamb and a magnetic, toothless grin that grew into a smile for everyone. She was easy-peasy and moved through the day usually glued to my right hip. We were a duo, going everywhere together. We made friends through playgroups and a variety of classes. Rachel was a great listener—cautious, smart, and kind. She loved people, playtime, and going to new places together.

I can still hear her say, "This one is Rachel-size, and this one is Mommy-size," as we strolled through the Gap or Bloomingdales looking at outfits. When she was older, she loved playing school and dressing up. Maybe that is what sparked her passion for fashion. She has always loved clothing. When she was four years old and had a sudden desire to dress herself every day, she often wore awful biking shorts; a Vail, Colorado, T-shirt; and a belt. But now she does have a knack for putting great outfits together.

Brian was born three years after Rachel. I was so consumed with Rachel that I had a difficult time connecting with Brian right away. His cry was loud like a lion, and he never slept. I must admit that there were a few weeks during his early days that Rachel and I weren't so thrilled with him. Fortunately, Kenny was.

One morning, I headed out for my post-pregnancy run. Brian and Kenny were hanging out in the kitchen—Brian in his Kanga Rockaroo and Kenny with his coffee and newspaper. When I got back, Kenny let me know that it was time for me to get to know my son. Of course, I was pissed when he said that, but as my breasts filled with milk and I could barely run two miles, I knew he was right. I needed to embrace my baby boy with the same sense of novelty and joy that I'd had when I first became a mother. In retrospect, I think I loved Rachel so much that I was afraid I didn't have the ability to love another child the same way.

Brian came into the world loving me, and I soon realized that my heart was full of love for this precious, red-headed, happy, curious, silly boy. I adored these little people who were the greatest gifts in my life. I have always said that I grew up with my kids and learned as much from them as they learned from me, but I had no idea how true that was until they moved back into our house in 2020 and the Lemonade Generation began.

My children are Millennials, born between 1981 and 1996. They grew up, went off to college, and then moved to New York City to conquer the world. We treasured their visits to Miami, packing every minute with fun and favorites in hopes they'd soon come back for more. Little did we know that their trip home in March 2020 with a one-way ticket would spark the BooMillennial Lab experiment of two generations living together for more than a year.

The world is changing, and I often joke, "We're not in Kansas anymore, but there is definitely no place like home."

March 12, 2020

"You're really wearing masks?" I asked Rachel and her boyfriend when I picked them up at the airport.

"These are the N-95 masks," Rachel's boyfriend said. "We left one with our doorman for Brian to pick up before he flies down tomorrow."

"He won't stop to pick it up," I said with an eye roll. "He's the fearless fool who jumped out of an airplane. Nothing scares him." Everyone was being so neurotic about this virus. I had just finished my to-do list so my slate would be clean and clear to enjoy the kids for the weekend. That list included selecting the menu and putting down the deposit for the bridal shower for Rachel's friend Libby, which was coming up on May 2, 2020. I also had to finalize all the plane tickets for our summer travel and submit two proposals to two new clients with timelines, travel expectations, and budgets. I was busy. The virus was in Asia, and really, this was not going to change my life one bit. *These kids are crazy!* I thought to myself.

Our children, better educated about COVID-19 than Kenny and I, were frustrated by our relaxed manner. Truth be told, we were probably in denial that something this monumental could really happen in our lifetime. We were so wrong, and they were so right. From minute one, our kids were laying down the rules about not going into the office, stopping all activities, shifting to grocery delivery, and becoming Amazon Prime experts. We were forbidden to go anywhere or see anyone. They acted as if we were super-senior citizens and that it was their responsibility to protect us from the virus. They even encouraged us to take large amounts of cash out of the bank just in case. In case of what? The kids did a good job of guilting us into shutting down while we had a myriad of questions and emotions looming in our minds.

We were not the only ones. In the beginning of the pandemic, everyone was asking each other what to do and what to think, although no one had answers for anything. We were all turning to each other for some sense of direction. During one of our early pandemic Zoom happy hours with our dear friends Karen and Robert, Karen shared: "It's so funny that my adult children have been so careful and proactive about their well-being, much more so than me. I take precautions, and I'm careful, but my kids make me feel like I'm a wild woman when I go to the grocery store or drugstore."

Karen and Robert were married on the same day as Kenny and I were—November 29, 1986—but we did not know each other then. We discovered this mutual celebration day twenty-five years ago and have celebrated together ever since. They are friends who became family. We have shared a lot of life together, but never before had we shared vodka in the Zoom room.

In just a few days, all our plans were canceled. We had no solutions, no control, no experience, and no leadership. We were truly winging it—just trying our best to stay healthy and safe while figuring out how to buy as much food, toilet paper, and essential items as possible.

Invaded by an invisible force, we were in combat with an illness, and we had very few weapons to defend ourselves and our loved ones.

The beginning was mayhem. We wiped every single item we brought into the house with Lysol. We wore bandanas as masks and dishwashing gloves on our hands everywhere we went.

The fear of touching and contracting the virus consumed us, and we believed we could somehow control it with our actions. No one had any answers about anything, not even my friend Ilene who always seemed to know the scoop, whether she really did or not. She couldn't even figure out how to get herself home to Miami from Sydney, Australia, and I thought she knew everything. But this was a global pandemic the likes of which hadn't been seen since the Spanish flu pandemic of 1918.

We spent our days working, cleaning, cooking, exercising, eating, and binging on the news—all without leaving the house. Siloed during the workday, we treasured the evenings when we convened as a family for dinner. We were lucky to be able to endure the craziness together while so many were stranded and separated from their loved ones.

For the first few weeks, I cooked every meal, fearful of bringing prepared food with germs into our home. When we went out for a walk, we wore masks, practiced social distancing, and washed our hands religiously. Mail and packages were left outside for twenty-four hours after delivery to air out any germs they carried. Kenny, still in denial about the severity of the virus, sighed with utter frustration regarding my newfound obsession with sanitization.

"Wash your hands!" I anxiously barked the minute he walked into the house. He would put down his briefcase and head directly to the kitchen sink where he proceeded to fluff up with an excessive amount of soap and rub his hands back and forth, front and back, surgical style for a ridiculous amount of time. That was my Kenny, the man who, even when I was out-of-control insane, found a way to bring humor to a mundane act such as washing his hands. He was definitely the last one to get on the coronavirus crazy train.

Three weeks in, we moved out of our comfortably spacious home into a rental apartment a few blocks away. We had recently sold our home and were in the process of building a new one. We had signed a lease for a two-bedroom, high-rise apartment where we would live for six months until our new house was ready. We had it all planned out pre-COVID, but suddenly all five members of our "Quaranteam" were moving together into our tiny rental. Rachel and her boyfriend took the second bedroom, and Brian slept in the open loft area adjacent to our bedroom. We set up a temporary folding wall to give him some personal space and used plastic bins as a pseudo-dresser where he could keep his belongings. Carving out a place to carry on his corporate professional role remotely was challenging. The three of us shared the upstairs bathroom where, on occasion, we found ourselves standing in line to pee in the middle of the night. Privacy was a rare commodity. "Shh" was the new foreplay in our bedroom. Seriously, you can't make this stuff up.

We had woes of Internet dysfunction, television tragedy, loud air conditioners, scary elevators, and a kitchen the size of a closet, but we made the best of it, and our pandemic routine continued. To keep things interesting, we started having themed dinners with creative cocktails, homemade desserts, table décor, and topics of conversation that coincided with the theme. Cinco de Mayo suddenly became a holiday in our home. We created a tacky, festive vibe with margaritas and a full taco buffet served on awful pink paper plates with cacti-plastered plastic cups and a flamingo centerpiece à la Amazon Prime.

"Turn up the music!" Rachel suggested with a grin, her hips moving in sync with the mambo. She successfully led all of us around our limited apartment space, turning a pathetic pandemic Tuesday into an instant fiesta. Rachel's sport has always been dance. She took dancing lessons from the age of three, and her annual recitals, fully adorned with costumes and makeup, always concluded with accolades, flowers, and ice cream. She loved the creativity and precision of dance. From a young age, Rachel's presence was illuminating, and her words were interesting and inspirational. She had a youthful wisdom and a unique zest for life in her core.

That night, something in my gut told me it was time to stop being the loudest voice in the room and focus on listening to those around me. I took the time to really absorb what my kids were saying and doing. I suddenly realized that I had a lot to learn from my Millennial children and that they were the proprietors of their lives and stories. That shift began my journey from Baby Boomer to BooMillennial. There we were, living in our own cauldron of collaboration, our unexpected living situation sparking moments of awareness and conversations about the relationship synergy organically occurring across the generations in our home.

Suddenly we were not the smart parents preaching to our young children. We were in a mutually beneficial, respectful adult relationship, and we had so much to absorb from one another that would enhance all our lives. It was clear that our adult children had a lot to say, and it was time for us to shut up and listen—and then listen some more.

2

Be the Air Dancer

Flexibility and Humor Make for a Happy Home

March 2020

Laura

It was a Friday in March 2020, and my son Andrew had just flown in from New York where the virus had already started to rear its ugly head. He'd been hearing rumblings of a city shutdown.

"Don't you think he's being a bit extreme?" my husband Dan asked me the previous night when we got Andrew's text that he was getting on a plane and coming home. We were in Miami walking our dog, and with the palm trees blowing in the breezy air, it was hard to imagine that this COVID-19 thing was real.

The next morning when I pulled up to United Airlines arrivals, Miami International Airport was eerily empty. My tall, adorable, twenty-six-year-old son was standing alone on the curb. He was wearing a hooded sweatshirt, a bag slung over his shoulder, and a surgical mask covering his face. I put the car in park and jumped out to give him a hug, but he instantly pulled away.

"Mom, you really need to put something over your face. I'm not kidding," he said urgently. I didn't own a face mask. Up until that moment I hadn't realized what was happening, but here was my son who would not hug me, had a mask on his face, and was hanging his head out the passenger window as we drove home. He was only a couple months into a new job, and now his company, like most other companies in New York, had closed its offices and was sending all personnel home indefinitely until further notice.

"I made a quick decision," he said. "I felt like there was a window of time when I could get a flight and leave the city, and I decided to make the move."

Years ago, a friend of mine had joked to me, "Don't worry about Andrew. He'll always get a seat on the subway." At that time, I was a young mom standing with other moms at the park, watching our children play. My friend could already see that Andrew was resourceful. With fair, freckled skin, blond hair, and a big, toothy smile, Andrew was the most delicious and delightful child. From the beginning, he seemed to be a practical, get-it-done kind of guy. I remember walking into the kitchen one morning, and there he was, no more than three years old, standing at the counter with a box of Entenmann's donuts trying to open the door to the microwave.

"Mommy, donut?" he asked.

"Sure. Why not?" I answered.

Andrew is and always has been authentically himself. He has a big, genuine personality, and like me, he is a middle child. We have always related well to each other.

But it had been almost eight years since he had lived full-time under our roof, and this was certainly going to be interesting. Our oldest son, Jacob (29), and his wife, Stephanie, were newlyweds, now living in Miami just a few miles away.

Our youngest, Emily (21), was in Michigan in her last semester of college.

I pulled the car into the driveway and watched as Andrew, the mask still on his face, walked into the house and went straight to the laundry room. He closed the door, stripped down to his underwear, and immediately put his clothes in the washing machine. He emerged moments later in a Miami Heat T-shirt and a pair of his old high school gym shorts. "What do you think if I set up my desk here—just for the time being?" he asked, plopping his backpack down by the dining room table and opening his laptop.

Little did we know that "the time being" would end up lasting an entire year.

As Andrew got to work at our dining room table, Dan grinned at me over his morning cup of coffee. "You need to be like one of those air dancers," he told me, swaying as he started to make his way out the door.

"What do you mean?" I asked with annoyance.

"You know," he said, "those inflatable nylon things—the ones that look like they're just completely flexible and dancing in the air."

Always my voice of reason, Dan was right. The image was perfect, and throughout the pandemic, it became my visual of what I tried to be—flexible, easygoing, and just dancing in the air. But although I tried, I was never one of those go-with-the-flow kind of mothers.

But back into our house our son came, now a professional going from working at 47th and Lexington Avenue in New York City to working virtually from our dining room table. It became immediately apparent that Dan and I were not the same people we had been when the kids left the house for college years earlier. We were older. We had become more set in our ways, and our lives had a different structure, or non-structure.

My days were no longer anchored by school drop-offs, pick-ups, and after-school practices where I'd linger in the school parking lot socializing and chatting. I had loved getting to know the other parents and seeing all the kids, and I was always thrilled to be buying snacks and fruit in bulk at Costco for friends who came over to the house. I remember my eyes welling up with tears as I stood in the grocery store the August Jacob left for college. I looked at the special on blueberries—two for the price of one—and realized that my blueberry-loving kid was no longer living at home.

For so many years I was my children's world—their driver, their chef, their magical mommy who could somehow always make it happen. I'd be up early every morning making breakfast before school, in the carpool line each afternoon, and even miraculously delivering the forgotten team uniform moments before the game. I cherished the days when we all sat at the dinner table together, when I heard the steady sound of the basketball bouncing on the driveway, when they were all home in our house, sleeping in their rooms. I felt secure in my role as their mother.

But eventually they all went away to college, and reluctantly I got used to a quiet house. And now suddenly we were in a pandemic, and pandemonium reigned with Andrew home again. Although it was great having one of my kids at home to cook for and take care of, neither of us was the same as when he had graduated from high school. Our son had returned home, only this time he was a grownup.

Andrew's workstation was set up right outside the kitchen door. At times I listened to him on his Zoom meetings and marveled at how intelligent, insightful, and articulate he was. At other times, he was so damn loud that I couldn't hear myself think. Our house, which had seemed so cavernous when the kids had all left, suddenly felt crowded. We had to learn to navigate new boundaries and figure out how to have new or maybe no expectations for our current state of cohabitation. And yet we knew we were the fortunate ones. We had a home and were able to take precautions to stay healthy, work remotely, and be together.

I tried to be sensitive to how Andrew must have been feeling. With the loss of in-person work, people could no longer spontaneously bump into a friend or have a random conversation with a colleague. What used to be a 4:00 p.m. conversation around the office water cooler had evolved to yet one more stroll to the kitchen—in sweatpants. Certainly this was not an ideal situation, yet Andrew knew how fortunate he was to have parents who welcomed him back home and even cooked for him. For Dan and me, it was fantastic to have someone available almost 24/7 to help with our frequent technology challenges. What so often stumps members of the Boomer generation is that Millennials and Gen Z-ers can figure it out in seconds. We became experts at adapting, keeping perspective, and above all, retaining our sense of humor.

My breakfast routine was instantly annoying to Andrew. After a few weeks of watching me make my "many-ingredient breakfast bowl with ten types of bird seed" as he called it, Andrew asked, "Mom, why don't you just put it all in one container so you don't have to mix it every day?"

He had a point, I suppose. But I like to keep my ingredients separate. "Why do you care?" I asked him.

After a few seconds of silence, we just looked at each other and cracked up. At the risk of losing it over flax seed, raspberries, and raisins, we just agreed to disagree. We were learning to "stay in our lanes," a term Andrew taught me early on in those first weeks of his homecoming. Eventually we became familiar with the protocol of mouthing these words: "Are you on the phone?" We mouthed that whenever one of us entered the other's territory. Like Cirque du Soleil gymnasts balancing on a tightrope, we were finding our footing.

For me, it was challenging to figure out when to speak and when to just keep my big motherly mouth shut. When the kids were little, I was like one of those wind-up toys—the oversized mouth that just bounces around, yapping its jaws until it exhausts itself. After several weeks of BooMillennial time together, I had to remember that my children were adults. I needed to control my mouth. No matter how brilliant or insightful I thought I was, I had to restrain myself from giving unsolicited advice. Andrew was an adult. If he wanted my opinion, he would ask.

One Saturday in the spring I was upstairs in my bedroom and heard the song "Born to Run" playing outside. Walking over to the window, I was surprised to see Dan, toolbox open, drill in hand, beer on the table, music turned up, in full afternoon Mr. Fix-It mode. He was building the outdoor hammock swing that had been sitting in a box in our garage since we moved into our new home over three years ago. *Good for him*, I thought.

Dan has always cherished the feeling of fulfillment that comes from building things, using his hands, and accomplishing tasks on his own. I had heard stories of when he and his brother were growing up in New York. They would be watching cartoons in their pajamas on a Saturday morning, and their father would say, "Boys, I need you." Whether it meant shoveling snow from the driveway or refurbishing something around the house, apparently there was no end to the home improvement projects that framed my husband's childhood. Just like his father before him, Dan now occasionally gives the one-line zinger—"Why would I pay someone else to do what I am perfectly capable of doing myself?" This inevitably produces big eye-rolling from our two adult sons who have often made me wonder if they've inherited any of their father's just-pick-up-the-shovel-and-help gene.

"Dad, do you realize you can hire a 'task rabbit,' and they would already be done by now?" That's what Andrew asked his dad after the fourth hour of hammock assembly.

"I don't want to hire someone else to do it," Dan snapped, rereading the instruction sheet yet again.

"I'm just saying. You're not as young as you think you are, Dad. It just seems like a waste of your time to do this all afternoon."

Ah, the joys of the honest conversations that played out in our household. The subtle and not-so-subtle comments made while living together hinted at the character traits our children hoped to inherit from us and those they would choose to leave behind.

"How are you going to know how to do things if you don't try to learn them?" Dan said later that afternoon while taking a break.

"What about the online marketplace and freelance labor for people who need work?" Andrew retorted. While it might have been inconsistent with the way things were done in previous generations, it was important for my husband to hear our Millennial son's well-supported views.

Andrew had been home living in our house for a few months when conversations about his future professional trajectory became more frequent. He had been working remotely for a New York–based real estate startup, and it was clear that the pandemic was already changing many things, including his intended career path. Over morning cups of coffee, nightly dinner conversations, and long dog walks, Andrew began to take interest in Dan's construction management company, pointing out ways he felt it could change and modernize.

"Dad, you could do so much better if you utilized technology," Andrew said, holding one end of the hammock as Dan secured the last bolts. While Dan knew Andrew was right, somehow it was not what he wanted to hear.

Eventually, Dan built the hammock to perfection, although it did take him almost until sundown to finish it. As we all sat outside later that night, Dan's legs dangling from the hammock, there was an unmistakable look of sublime satisfaction on his face. Or as Andrew said, maybe he was just preparing himself for the miserable backache he knew would be inevitable in the morning.

Andrew was right. Although it was becoming difficult to accept, we were not those vibrant youngsters anymore. We were, in fact, getting older, and old dogs must force themselves to learn new tricks and open those aging minds to new ideas, no matter how difficult it may seem. We were quickly learning that not only did we need to make room in our house, but we also needed to make space for different opinions and other viewpoints. I was never the type of parent who could completely back off and say to my kids, "Sure, do whatever you think. That's fine with me." Instead, I had a tendency to hover—big time.

I got married young and had my babies in the '90s, smack in the middle of the prime time "helicopter parenting" era when overly present and overly involved parenting was in vogue. Many pregnant mothers in the 1980s and

1990s followed every word of Heidi Murkoff's book *What to Expect when You're Expecting.* It was "the pregnancy bible" for expectant mothers. Many moms like me were in the habit of checking every milestone of our infant's developmental progress. This habit continued when the child entered preschool, and before you knew it, we were scrutinizing every test score and sport stat.

In the 1980s in the United States, women were beginning to thrive in their careers, and the median age of first-time marriages began to tick up. It was the era of the empowered woman. While in some circumstances economic realities dictated employment, this was the first time many women had a choice. They could stay on the professional track or stay at home and be a full-time mom. Women were making their own choices, trying to figure out what worked best for their families as well as their own personal and professional goals.

Before kids and after studying journalism and communications in college at Indiana University, I moved to New York City. I soon met Dan, the man who would become my husband. Four years later, after my short stint in advertising, we moved to Miami. Although I was thrilled to be back home living near my family, I had not even scratched the surface in deciding what career and parenting path would ultimately be best for me.

On New Year's Eve in 1991, I was eight months pregnant with our first child. Standing in the kitchen making spinach dip to bring to a friend's party, I felt those first twinges in my belly. *This can't be it,* I thought. *My due date isn't for another few weeks.*

Forget the dip and the New Year's Eve party. Ready or not, baby Jacob was born about an hour and a half after I was admitted to the hospital that night. He weighed in at

6 pounds, 1 ounce. Dan started calling family and friends. "Happy New Year! We have a baby boy!" There were jokes about the last-minute tax deduction, and soon my parents were in my hospital room with a bottle of champagne. Deliriously elated, Dan and I ushered in 1992 as new parents.

The following Monday morning, I watched as Dan's car rolled out of the driveway and he headed back to his office. With a still-big, post-pregnancy belly and an ugly short hair-cut, I was quite a sight as I stood there in my pink bathrobe holding our newborn, tears streaming down my face. I felt as though my world had turned upside down. At 27, how had I suddenly gone from account executive in the frenetic, fast-paced world of advertising to full-time mommy? Yes, of course I'd had (almost) nine months to prepare for this, but here it was, and I was a mess. There was so much else I thought I should be doing. Instead, I was steeped in the minutia of this baby's life, already feeling the fatigue of never having a moment to myself. It felt as if there was a whole world going on outside, and I could barely find my shoes, much less figure out how to open the stroller and get out there.

I don't remember if the term postpartum depression was a thing back then, but I definitely had some version of it. How was it that one minute I could be sitting there holding my son, beaming with pride at this beautiful, healthy baby boy, and the very next second I was crying for the old life I used to have? No one tells you how difficult it is to make the transition from just taking care of yourself to becoming the caretaker of another human being, no matter how adorable and delicious that little being may be. You can read all the parenting books and blogs, but nothing prepares you for the reality of motherhood.

The next twenty years or so went by in a blur. Dan and I were prime examples of the build-self-esteem, participation-trophy movement. We immersed ourselves in our three kids' activities and interests, hanging on to every word they shared and being there for all the victories and disappointments.

My parents did it differently. My vivid memories of when I was a kid back in the Mad Men era were of my mother—hair done, lipstick on, dressed in a fuchsia and orange printed dress—serving my father his half-grapefruit appetizer for dinner. Their relationship was her focus, and my mother will tell you unabashedly that my two sisters and I were bathed, fed, and in bed "without any discussion" by 7:30 every night. In contrast, when my children were little, the bedtime hour was more like a Broadway musical or an episode of *Law and Order* with stories, songs, and elaborate negotiations before winding down the day.

My mother, like most mothers in the 1960s, didn't overthink her parenting choices. She didn't spend hours and hours analyzing and evaluating every little move her children made. Instead, she followed the advice of Dr. Benjamin Spock, the American pediatrician who wrote the landmark 1946 book *Dr. Spock's Baby and Child Care*. I grew up in Miami, Florida, the middle child of three sisters. Our parents were happy for my sisters and me to be outside playing in the neighborhood all afternoon. While we were usually at the dinner table together every night, there was little concern about what we were doing before dinner or what random teenage acts we would be partaking in after dinner. If I needed to get to an after-school activity or practice, I did not rely on my parents to get me there.

My father, an attorney, went to the office every day, and my mother, though home most afternoons after school, was busy doing whatever it was mothers of that generation did. For me, my sisters, and our friends, there was never any expectation that our parents would be around to shuttle us from place to place. As a 10-year-old, I walked myself down the block to my friend's house to play. As a 12-year-old, I hopped on my powder blue Schwinn 10-speed bike and rode to the tennis court or soccer field. I was mobile.

On weekends, my friends and I arranged for one mother to drop us off at the mall or the roller-skating rink and another to pick us up. "Be outside and ready at 5:45," she would say, unconcerned if that time worked well for me or not. There was no "text me and let me know if you girls want me to come later" or anything absurd like the hoops I would jump through three decades later as I sat idly in my car with snacks and drinks at the ready and a stack of reading material, killing time while waiting as long as necessary for my children, those little majesties, to emerge from their activity or team practice.

My parents went out on weekends and left us kids at home with a babysitter. As my mother, Dorothy, reminds my sisters and me, she didn't get too hung up on checking babysitters' references. "Any teenager with a pulse," we all joked years later. There were no cell phones with apps like Find My Friends. With inexperienced babysitters and Swanson frozen dinners on our TV trays, we grew up watching the Saturday night TV lineup of shows that any kid of the '70s can recite. It was a simpler time. We were fortunate that our parents were able to take us on great summer trips, driving across the country to see the national parks. My sisters and I all sat in the back seat of our station wagon, me in the middle. We sang along with the eight-track player to familiar show tunes as we weaved our way through the canyons. *Hello Dolly, Camelot, Oklahoma*—we knew all the songs.

As we got older, our parents were busy focusing on themselves and the things they needed to do. They let us lead our own lives. I attended a huge Miami public school with a diverse population where somehow the students coexisted.

Everyone seemed to find their own place and make space for each other. Friday nights under the lights, football was everything. Heading into the 1980s, we were all aspiring to be part of the *Miami Vice* lifestyle.

When I went away to college, I called my parents long distance from a pay phone once a week and sent snail mail to stay connected with family and friends. My parents wanted what was best for me, but they were not obsessed with my life. They allowed me to make my own choices and be responsible for my own mistakes.

In contrast, many parents of my generation became busy planning everything in their children's lives. As over-scheduling became an accepted way to raise families, the sense of balance was often lost. In retrospect, many of us have begun to ask ourselves if our Millennial children were burned out, disillusioned, and unprepared for the world that awaited them. Or did our extreme involvement help them grow into the decisive, smart adults that they are?

When our daughter, Emily—our "baby"—left for college, it was hard to adjust. We had found such fulfillment in our kids' lives and their accomplishments that, like many empty nesters, Dan and I had to readjust our lives. We had to learn to create new, less interdependent relationships with our children.

I remember the first day of Emily's college years. We pulled into Ann Arbor, Michigan, with her duffle bags in the trunk of the rental car. On that August day, the campus was alive with college kids milling about as far as the eye could see. We parked the car, and the three of us began lugging Emily's boxes of books and supplies up the stairs. We organized her desk as we made cheery conversation with the other parents who were all similarly scurrying around. Dan assembled the portable plastic containers that would hold Emily's new seafoam green towels and slid the drawers under the bed. I unpacked the three throw pillows—one lilac, one seafoam, and one an image of a cool artistic landscape that Emily had found online. The color palette of these pillows had occupied a disproportionate amount of our discussion time during the weeks leading up to this moment, as if to avoid the reality of the elephant in the room that our last child was leaving the nest.

Dan's mom, Judi, has six grandchildren. Emily is the youngest. At birth, each child got a handmade blankie cross-stitched with "xoxo with love from Nanny." Before each child left for college, Nanny made it her tradition to take them shopping at Bed, Bath and Beyond for the bedding, towels, and toiletries they'd need at college. I don't remember Jacob or Andrew picking throw pillows on this ritual outing when they left for college. Yet the queasy stomach and the steadily building ache of anticipation were unmistakable each time. Will they still need me?

I carefully tucked in the sheets, smoothed the comforter, and arranged the pillows on Emily's bed. She put the two framed photos of our family and one of the dogs on the little shelf above her desk and took out a stack of photos of her friends, which she planned to tape to the wall above her bed. We met her roommate, a lovely and seemingly industrious, independent young lady who had traveled by herself all the way from New Delhi, India. It was time for me to realize that my daughter had grown up, and I had to learn to let go.

3

Paralyzed in Our Sweatpants

Reframe Your Reality

April 2020

Adrian

I loved that his scent was so fresh and familiar. My husband Kenny was beautifully suited up, down to his Italian loafers. Although some days his routine was slightly varied, his norm was to pause in the kitchen for a kiss goodbye before heading out to his office that had been in the same location for over forty years.

"What's on your schedule today?" he asked while quickly walking toward the front door.

"Full day, but I can't wait to see you tonight," I replied. I didn't mean to be aloof, but we lived independent lives and enjoyed our time together as well.

Kenny left for his workplace where he accomplished his daily professional commitments, enjoyed interoffice camaraderie, and had deep friendships. He appreciated the bonding experience of working day after day, year after year with like-minded professionals who continued to evolve for the best interests of their clients and the organization. When the pandemic brought lock-down into our lives, this routine came to a very sudden stop. It was tax season, and Kenny was adamant that his presence was necessary in the office. He was somewhat in denial that COVID was really happening, even though Dr. Anthony Fauci was constantly stressing on TV the importance of following the stay-at-home guidelines and insisting that everyone, even the busiest of professionals, comply with the rules.

Change has never been easy for my husband, but it was time to take off the suit, put on the sweatpants or shorts with appropriately professional Zoom attire from the waist up, and go to work in our bedroom.

During the pandemic, Kenny spent approximately twen-ty-one hours per day in our bedroom. His office was two Home Depot tables right next to our bed. He only came out of the bedroom for meals, exercise, and maybe a few hours of TV time in the evening.

My desk consumed the middle of the living room. Even though I wore earbuds or earplugs while trying to focus, I could still hear Ken's loud voice through the wall. And our son, Brian, conducted his business in his unique office-bedroom with his adjustable standing desk, swivel chair, and a variety of screens all pinging at the same time. This quickly became our normal, and our normal was much easier than what many families were experiencing. The work-from-home phenome-non for many included not only home offices but also virtual schooling for all ages, laundry piles growing higher, drivers delivering food, domestic care shrinking for fear of bringing another person into the house—and all this took place at the same address for the entire family.

Prior to the pandemic, most people worked in a physi-cal location outside their home, which made for a division of space and focus. Then COVID-19 arrived, and the rapid shift to working from home just happened. There was no warning, no rulebook, and no alternate plan.

Thirty years ago, the word *zoom* was a verb that meant "to move very quickly." When Brian was little, he would set up his toy cars and say in his deepest voice, "zoom, zoom!" as he moved the cars around the racetrack that had a permanent spot in our playroom. Sometimes when we were driving together and I would pass another car, he would shout, "zoom, zoom!" from his car seat, enjoying the feeling of the acceleration of my car. As a young mommy, I often "zoom zoomed" on the road when I was rushing to complete all my tasks before I picked up my kids from school or one of their weekly activities. Rushing to be on time for my kids was deeply rooted in my psyche. Never wanting to be the "late mommy," I was committed to arriving on time for my children as well as for most of the commitments I made in my life. Time was precious, cherished, and scarce, even more so when I shifted from being a timely mommy to giving my time to the nonprofit world.

It was 1996, and I was standing in the middle of the family room of my new post-Hurricane Andrew home four years after the storm. As the board meeting ended and we began to bring the coffee cups and crumb-filled plates into the kitchen, I heard my friend Robyn say in a tone filled with passion, responsibility, and determination, "It's time."

"It's time for what?" I asked, confused. At first I thought, *Am I late picking up my kids from nursery school?* But it was only 11:00 a.m., and pickup time was at 11:45, giving me 30 minutes before I had to leave home for the ten-minute commute. What was I missing? I was so happy to host the monthly board meeting. We had been displaced for over a year post-hurricane. Enough furniture had arrived to make the house look lived in, even though the living room was empty except for the baby grand piano and the kids' overflow of toys.

In my navy, houndstooth pants and simple navy sweater, I was happy to do my part to help the mission of the organization. The ladies, all beautifully groomed, strolled into the house for our two-hour meeting, leaving with enough time to get into the carpool line for nursery pickup and their afternoon full of work, activities, and errands. Robyn was determined to continue the conversation even though the ladies were leaving, and I was a bit frenzied to put away the bagels and fruit and get the kitchen somewhat organized before I had to pick up my little people.

"It's time, Adrian," Robyn repeated. "It's time for you to take a leadership role in our community. This is your community now."

"Okay," I replied vaguely as the pleaser that I am, not fully understanding her message but knowing it was important.

Eventually, I realized that Robyn was honoring my strengths and inviting me to join a nonprofit leadership journey that in the years to come would fill my life with great people, purpose, and passion.

My friend Laura—and now co-author—was one of the young mommies who rushed from the meeting at my house to get in the carpool line to pick up her son Andrew. She cared deeply about the challenges in our world and gave of herself with a heart filled with kindness and compassion.

Both Laura and I are women filled with gratitude. Over the years, we have paused to discuss where this similar sense of appreciation comes from, and after many lengthy processing conversations, we often concluded that it flows in our DNA. We are connectors, doers, and givers. We like to be productive—a trait we inherited from our Virgo mothers—and we like accomplishing the mission. Our parents and grandparents were role models for us as children and young adults. As young mothers, we realized that it was our turn to step up and begin our journey into the nonprofit volunteer world. We needed something in our lives to stimulate our mushy mommy brains and help us focus on the needs of others outside our immediate families. We each took on leadership positions with various organizations, and as our children grew up, our friendship grew deeper, and we became advisory women in our community.

My nonprofit journey began that day in the kitchen with Robyn, and now, twenty years later in the same kitchen, Laura and I tossed salads and opened bottles of wine to prepare for our Good Works Miami, LLC launch gathering. This time the house was in disarray with moving boxes and stacks of items to donate. Kenny and I had sold our home since Brian was just finishing college and Rachel had already begun her career in New York City. We were building an "empty nester" house in a more urban part of town.

Many of the same well-groomed women from 22 years ago were invited to attend a focus group at my dining room table that would allow us to share our visions and hear feedback regarding what everyone's volunteer interests were and what gave them fulfillment in life. The women were candid. We learned that some loved tennis, golf, and Mahjong, while others had returned to their full-time professions. Some wanted a more structured and consistent volunteer opportunity, and others preferred flexibility and participating when it worked best for their schedules. Overall, the consensus was that they wanted to live purposeful lives.

Laura and I are both passionate about service and community. Grateful for the leadership training and opportunities we have had over the years, we have witnessed firsthand the tremendous joy of giving back and the fulfillment of making a difference in the lives of others. Our goal has been to leverage what we have learned to help organizations optimize their potential, people, and purpose. While this is work we have each been doing for more than thirty years, living during the pandemic gave us insight into the nuances of the rapidly changing nonprofit world and the challenges the next generation is facing. We were realizing in real time that we needed to evolve, grow, and identify how we could add value and mentor new leaders to lead organizations going forward. "It's time" are powerful words that keep evolution in motion. How quickly we've zoomed through the years, now finding ourselves in the popular Zoom room—the Zroom.

During the COVID era, thousands of professionals like Kenny turned Home Depot 72-inch folding tables into bedroom office desks. Back pain set in from sitting on a folding chair for hours on end. And we ordered multiple monitors as face-to-face became Zoom-to-Zoom.

One day a client said to me, "I have to get off this call. I have Zoom hips."

"I have Zoom neck," I replied, and we both laughed, relieved to be honestly sharing these challenges.

Too much "ass-in-the-chair" sitting had become a thing. People were settling into a new way of life, learning to be comfortable with the uncomfortable and beginning to acknowledge that although not ideal, our virtual world was efficient. There was no commuting or travel time, and the turnaround time from one meeting to the next was almost seamless. But the pandemic also illuminated the inequities in our world.

Zoom opened our eyes to each other's living situations in a way that perhaps we had not previously understood. We had a unique window into a more real version of people's day-to-day lives—awkward backgrounds on the Zoom view and all. While some people had highly staged and well-curated backdrops, others struggled to find a quiet corner or space in a closet, adapting in real time to less-than-ideal working environments and unpredictable connectivity issues. People were patient with each other as we navigated this new technical territory together.

It's amazing how quickly I became acclimated to working at home while wearing my loyal, stretchy sweatpants and throwing on a pearl necklace with a black T-shirt to set the professional tone for the Zoom of the hour. Occasionally, I made myself try on a pair of jeans, reassuring myself that they still fit. As Dr. Fauci spoke with conviction about lowering the curve of the pandemic, I felt my pandemic curves bulging larger!

Pre-pandemic, more women than ever before held both essential and high-level professional positions in our country. The question of what defined an "essential" job came up for the first time. Women also led the charge regarding child-rearing, domestic tasks, nutrition, hygiene, and emotional, physical, and psychological well-being for spouses, partners, children, parents, friends, and, when time allowed, themselves.

The stress and anxiety that mothers felt was irrefutable. My daughter Rachel's dear friend Monica, an extraordinarily vivacious and successful dietician and first-time mother, was thrilled when she was finally able to put her son in daycare, sharing that her clients did not find it as cute as her husband's business colleagues did when their one-year-old wandered into the room during a Zoom meeting. She stressed how unfair it is that women are expected "to do it all without any indication of the other responsibilities in their lives, but a man with a baby is cute."

"Pre-pandemic, I often fantasized about working from home," Alison, a fellow board member, told me on a Zoom call one day. "But in my fantasy, the rest of the family was not home with me every day with their own daily agendas to accomplish. It was an overwhelmingly daunting task shifting to the new work-from-home status. My personal time became my professional time, and vice versa, as life was all happening at the same time."

My super-organized, moderately uptight younger friend Lauren, who worked from home while her elementary-age children attended virtual school, shared this with me: "My days are consumed with making sure the kids are in front of their computers learning and interacting with their classes and teachers. The other day, I found my five-year-old son playing video games in another room while his kindergarten class was in full motion. This was taking place while I was trying to lead a client meeting on Zoom. I'm skimming through my days, not accomplishing what is expected of me professionally or as a parent—and forget about trying to be a romantic partner. There is no time to even think about shaving my legs, let alone having sex. After all, who would even want to be intimate with me? I spend my day in sweatpants and only put lipstick on for a Zoom meeting. I have to prioritize my job because we need the money, and no one in the Zoom world can see that I no longer fit into my adorable work clothes. I spend my days on multitask overload."

Early in the pandemic when the lockdown began, many women received a notice of job termination or furlough. Women working in industries such as hospitality, travel, education, domestic care, and retail were greatly affected. Women lost more than 5.4 million jobs, accounting for more than half of the job losses in the United States. When the world shut down, the unemployment catastrophe began, having the greatest effect on women of color.

Women also disappeared from the workplace by quitting. As women faced the increase in domestic responsibilities that came from daycare closures, virtual school, and sick family members, they often had no choice but to quit and face the financial consequences. *The New York Times* featured an article about domestic workers "ghosted" by their employers. Many families were afraid to have their domestic helpers in their homes, fearful that they would bring in the virus. Some households did not even notify their domestic workers; they just ghosted them. My heart aches from this insensitivity toward those who cared for their homes and most precious possessions.

The stay-at-home shift impacted every profession, but women were affected more than men because women are like the Nike slogan—we just do it. We are heavy lifters. We make it happen for everyone. We seem to be hardwired to tune in to the needs of others. At a young age, women learn to care for their dolls and their siblings. They make things pretty, like ponytails with bows and coordinated outfits. They like fluffy objects and pleasing colors. They like to play school and teach others. They are born to take charge and make nice while accomplishing everything a boy does in the classroom and the board room. They are multitaskers by nature. This is what their foremothers modeled for them to different degrees for generations. Women work while managing households, their children's routines, often their significant other's extracurricular schedule, and in some cases their aging parents' lives. Women take care of those they love.

My mother always worked professionally, which was unusual for mothers of her generation. She was a pioneer of the work-from-home practice, caring for her family and volunteering in her community while running a business at the same time. After school, my brother and I hung out in the family room with our bowls of cereal for a snack, watched the allowed 30 minutes of TV—usually *The Andy Griffith Show*, *The Beverly Hillbillies*, *Hogan's Heroes*, or *Gomer Pyle, U.S.M.C.*—before heading off to an after-school activity. Mom would pop in from her basement office to give kisses, discuss our day, and make sure we felt her presence.

Occasionally, Mom would be out at a meeting, and her secretary would fill in for her at home. We thought this was normal. When she was really in a bind and needed more extensive childrearing help, she dropped us off at the most wonderful place in town—our grandma's house. Grandma had no rules and lots of love. She provided us with comfort and security like no other. She enjoyed us at least as much as we enjoyed her, and I believe Grandma enjoyed her grandchildren's childhood more than raising her own children. It was a different time in her life and a different time in the world.

My first cousin Sheila was often my playmate at Grandma's house since her mother, Aunt Babs, was also a working mom. Sheila grew up to become a child and family therapist, and she and I have spent many hours together processing our childhoods. We know how fortunate we were to have this incredible little lady as our grandma.

Grandma was a giver who gave unconditional love to her family and always believed in doing what she could for others. She baked Mandel bread for her neighbors, especially Mr. Calderello, the Italian man next door who loved Grandma's Jewish version of biscotti. Grandma loaned money to Elenora, her housekeeper, because she needed the money more than Grandma did. As a young child, I watched Grandma put money in a tin collection box every week for "those families who are not able to do for themselves." This was her language, and I have quoted her many times over the years during my nonprofit journey.

Like my parents, my grandma gave in ways that were meaningful to her. I was aware of their community involvement, but not until I was told that "it was time" for me to take the lead did I understand how important succession in leadership could be.

In 2020 when so many in our world were suffering, my own kids began to show me how Millennials give and lead organically. They have been elbow-deep in community service since they were very young. Mitzvah, or good deed projects, were the norm. As a family, we made peanut butter and jelly sandwiches for the homeless, planted trees in Israel, and sang songs to the elderly who were living in state-funded facilities.

At the age of thirteen, Rachel organized a 5K race at a local park to benefit an organization that provides comfort and care for children who have lost a parent or significant loved one. She did this in memory of my brother, Brent, who died at the age of thirty-five, leaving a wife and two young daughters. When Rachel left for college, Brian took her race to the next level. They did their "good stuff" in their own way, which is very different from mine.

When kids are little, they think their parents know best. After all, parents are the adults. As time goes by, however, our children become independent thinkers with their own opinions. Isn't that ultimately what we want? During the COVID period, I began to see that as badly as Laura and I wanted to tie everything up in pretty pink ribbon and repair the world, our kids didn't need us to be the "fixers" in their lives. They had their own paths to live happy, meaningful, generous, loving, experience-filled, financially secure lives.

My heart ached one night as our son Brian shared with us at the dinner table that he was not inclined to work for the same stable company for 40-plus years like his father had. He told us he had been giving it a lot of thought and was going to make some changes. He was going to carve his own professional path while traveling the world, running marathons, making others happy, and experiencing life to the fullest.

This was my instant reaction: *What did we do wrong? He's living in la-la land!* The unknown scares me, and my usual course of action is to follow the path of least resistance with a touch of terrain changes to keep life interesting. What's wrong with the road less rocky? I was dumbfounded by Brian's professional intentions. What do we do when we have encouraged our kids to be the best version of themselves and that turns out to be someone we don't know?

Kenny gently pushed my jaw shut when my mouth was stuck in the OMG open position while I listened to Brian casually discuss his plans. My thoughts went back to both my mom and my grandmother who had lived through tremendous change and rocky terrain and accepted it all with hearts full of love. Why was this so difficult for me? Was I overly invested in Brian's decisions and successes? Now he was making life's decisions without me. I am totally obsessed with my son and want the best for him, but do I really know what is best for him? Perhaps it was time for me to acknowledge that he is an extremely bright young man who has always figured things out. It was time for me to relax in the certainty that this, too, he will figure out.

4

Release

Embrace What You Can't Control

May 2020

Laura

Emily, my youngest child, is part of Gen Z, those born between 1997 and 2012. The last time she had been home was in the first week of March 2020, before we knew we were in a pandemic. She had invited six of her friends—all seniors at the University of Michigan—to come down to Miami for spring break. Thrilled to be thawing out from the winter, they relaxed on the beach and bounced from club to club, blissfully unaware of the virus somewhere out there. On the Sunday morning before they left, it occurred to me that I should probably get them some antibacterial wipes before they boarded the plane.

The scene at Walgreens that morning resembled the pre-hurricane mayhem we Floridians have become so accustomed to. In utter panic, everyone scrambles to the grocery store to grab anything they can get their hands on. I didn't know then how big of a score that three-pack of Lysol wipes was and how I would later reflect with gratitude on my good fortune as I carefully rationed those wipes for weeks. With big hugs, the spring breakers headed back to college for the final portion of their college experience. Who knew that just weeks later, the world would change completely?

"Mom, with all due respect, I don't see why I have to come home," Emily texted from campus one day in early April.

I texted her back. "Because, Emily, the country is in lockdown. It's freezing cold in Michigan. I don't know which flights will be going out of there, and if you get sick, I don't know how I will be able to get to you." I was aware that my full-on drama-mama, panic-mode self was coming through loud and clear. I knew that Emily's "with all due respect" probably meant she was sitting on the couch surrounded by her friends who were all sharing similar texts with their mothers.

"I'm not trying to be rude, Mom," she continued, "but I'm not sure what it is you think you're going to be able to do for me if I get sick."

She had a point. What would I actually be able to do? Who even knew what any of us were supposed to be doing in this situation? *Unprecedented* was the word we kept hearing on the news. Nothing like this had ever happened in our lifetime, and I was completely freaking out. Who could blame Emily for not wanting to end her college experience this way? A month before graduation with no job lined up and no adequate time to say her goodbyes, Emily was being asked to come home. I felt awful. Unprecedented or not, she was adamant that she had no intention of leaving school early and moving back into our house.

Since Emily had two older brothers, she had learned early on how to hold her own. When I was pregnant with her and already the mother of two young boys, I never quite admitted to myself how deeply I'd hoped it would be a girl. And then Emily was born. I had a daughter! I dressed her in pink and brought her home to her feminine, frilly room. Thinking back on it now seems comical because almost from minute one, Emily made it her mission to try to keep up with her brothers.

My husband Dan was a volunteer coach of Emily's soccer team. He set the orange cones across the field and practiced dribbling drills with a bunch of kindergarten kids who usually seemed more interested in snacks than soccer. Having been a competitive swimmer throughout high school and college, Dan innately understood what it meant to make a commitment to a team. He taught each of our children at an early age that it didn't matter whether they were the best athlete; what was most important was giving their best effort. He taught them how to be on time for practice, show respect, and honor the coach's rules, even if they didn't necessarily agree with them. With rolling eyes, the kids would joke when their dad would repeat the old adage passed down from his own college swimming coach—"the Five Ps: proper preparation prevents piss-poor performance." Life's lessons played out on the court, and the ballfield became a precursor for our kids' navigating their working lives and the hierarchy of the professional world.

Whatever sport or game the boys played, Emily wanted to play with them. Dressed in the basketball shorts she had stolen from their closets, as well as some elbow and knee pads, she taught herself at six years old how to "drop in" on her skateboard, whizzing up and down the sides of the half-pipe as my husband egged her on with pride. She stood there with her skateboard teetering over the edge of the half-pipe, aware that her brothers' eyes were on her as she calculated the exact timing to put her weight on the front of the board and let herself fly forward. She was fearless. She had more guts at age six than

I did at forty. This little blonde-haired beauty had so much spunk, sass, and creativity that I couldn't believe she was actually my daughter. How do you celebrate that? How could I just let her be her, not get in the way, and not try to control her or mold her into what I or society thought that she needed to be?

Emily has always followed her own gut and done things her own way. So it was not surprising that she pushed back when it came to COVID restrictions after the Governor of Michigan issued this statewide stay-at-home order:

> To suppress the spread of COVID-19, to prevent the state's health care system from being overwhelmed, to allow time for the production of critical test kits, ventilators, and personal protective equipment, and to avoid needless deaths, it is reasonable and necessary to direct residents to remain at home or in their place of residence to the maximum extent possible.

After two weeks and many sleepless nights, I booked my daughter a one-way ticket from Detroit to Miami. Emily tried to conceal her tears on the phone as we began to go through the logistics of her packing up, finding an N95 face mask, and getting a ride to the airport to come home. She was an art student and had been working for months on her senior project. Now, since there would be no in-person exhibit as originally planned, she needed to quickly accelerate her work so she could photograph it before disassembling it and cleaning out her studio—her coveted workspace she had aspired to as a sophomore and junior in the art program. She and her friends quickly got busy packing duffle bags, cleaning closets, and loading car trunks. They filled their social media feeds with pictures from impromptu graduation photo shoots where they tried desperately to hold onto a moment in time that was slipping away much too quickly.

For the class of 2020, the realization was becoming all too clear that life was not going to be what anyone expected. Emily's graduation from college would be different than we had all hoped for. Like so many parents trying to mark this milestone for my child, I went straight into we-will-make-the-very-best-of-it mode. I ordered decorations and signs and, with her roommates' mothers, made photo tributes and a video montage. Graduation took place on a computer screen in our backyard with all five of us and our dog, Louie, gathered around Emily. We made a socially distanced backyard barbeque with cakes and champagne, and we toasted to our graduate who, despite the disappointment of not having the kind of celebration she had anticipated, shifted gears and embraced the day. We all focused on gratitude for our family's health and for being together with the people we most cared about.

Mothers of teenage daughters know that navigating those moody years is not for the faint of heart. I was not prepared to encounter that old life all over again with my twenty-one-year-old daughter. Just when I thought I had left the phase of one-syllable answers and rolling eyes behind, 2020 brought a middle school aura right back into our house. Emily's bedroom door once again seemed to return to a default setting of closed, exuding a "don't you even think about knocking on this door" vibe. The three other adults in the house who had finally figured out the COVID-19 choreography of living and working together were not prepared for the twenty-one-year-old who had just joined us, emerging from her bedroom those first few weeks right around noon. As Emily walked into the kitchen, she would ask incredulously, "There's no more coffee?"

Andrew and I would exchange glances and then quickly look away, both of us careful not to get caught by her discerning eye. During those post-graduation weeks of lying on the sofa in her pajamas and doing freelance logo designs from her childhood bedroom, Emily's emotions were running high. We were all doing our best to make space for each other, and everyone in the house was working hard to find their footing.

At the same time, our oldest son Jacob and his wife Stephanie—just newly married—were now living in lockdown a few miles away. I was grateful they were living nearby. In the spring of 2020, my Sunday afternoon phone conversations with them were often the same. "Do you want to come for dinner?" I asked. "What time is good for you guys, and what should we order?"

Jacob and Steph had met each other ten years earlier, right after high school graduation. From that summer on, they had been basically inseparable. It was a unique situation to have your nineteen-year-old son know with such certainty that this was his person. And with a mother's instinct, I knew from the very beginning that they belonged together.

Fast forward through their college graduations and the few years they lived separately but both in New York to the time when Jacob moved to Miami and enrolled in law school. A year later he orchestrated a fantastic surprise with both families together to celebrate their engagement. A year and a half later, it felt like a dream to watch them dance at their beautiful wedding. Then in an instant, 2020 arrived, necessitating a readjustment to the reality of life. Now the newlyweds were navigating this new virtual world, living and working from their laptops with little balance to their days.

While I knew that any hardships they were experiencing paled compared to so many others, lockdown was a curveball for them. Their apartment building with its elevators and public spaces was a source of concern. Our spontaneous week-night meals and Sunday dinners were a blessing, allowing us to come together and check in on each other. From the very beginning of the pandemic, there was never a week we did not get to see them. Compared to some of my other friends whose kids lived far away, I knew I was very fortunate, yet I couldn't stop worrying.

"Do you hug them?" my friend Dianne asked me.

"I do," I said, wondering if she thought I was being irresponsible.

None of us knew what the right answers were. Personally, I felt the emotional benefits of hugging with masks on our faces outweighed the risks of spreading the virus. I needed to hug my children. Often, I was so elated to be able to see them that I went way over the top, cooking two or even three entrees just in case they wanted choices. I sent them home with containers of leftovers—my thought was that food could somehow off-set the social isolation of their lives. I found myself worrying. Were they happy? Were they depressed? Were they too much in each other's space? I scrutinized their expressions as if looking for clues to solve a mystery. Was my son wearing the same T-shirt he had worn two days ago? How often were they doing laundry, and why did I care?

"I am in full-on neurotic helicopter mother mode," I told my friend Susan one day when we were talking on the phone. I had known Susan for years. She was a social worker, community advocate, and grandmother who had two daughters a few years older than my kids. She always had great advice on how not to put your own "stuff" on your adult children. Susan was spending much of the spring of 2020 with her husband in what could be called a generational pandemic Petri dish.

She laughed as she told me about those first few weeks in their home in New York, rotating visits from her two adult daughters, their husbands, and her grandchildren.

"Merging three generations together under one roof was challenging to say the least," she said. "I knew I was going to have to let go of any illusions of control." She spent the first few days simmering, trying to get everyone to care about tidying up. Then with work schedules, meal prep, and logistics, she said the light bulb went off pretty early in their time together, and it crystallized. It was like that scene in the movie *Father of the Bride* when Steve Martin is running from the Dobermans and screams, "Release!"

Susan said, "I realized if they didn't care about cleaning up to my standards, who cares? Why should I make this conversation a focus of my mother-child relationship? It's about shifting gears and embracing whatever comes."

It was great advice, the kind I needed. This time was forcing everyone to shift gears. So maybe my son Jacob was wearing the same shirt—again. Who wasn't?

This time was making me more empathetic to the challenges my children were facing. For them, as for so many others, there was no delineation to their workdays, which often began at 7:30 a.m. Twelve hours later, they would still be on their computers, finishing things or beginning new assignments that had just come in. The expectation in the new virtual world was for immediate turnaround. It felt like a never-ending workday, which didn't include any real social contact with friends or colleagues. As the days and weeks slowly passed, I learned that since I had no control, I just had to let go of my expectations and release.

5

Sustenance for Survival

Gratitude Is an Essential Ingredient for Life

June 2020

Adrian

My grandma was a good baker, but her inventory of sweets was limited and simple—mandel bread, white powder cookies, and oatmeal raisin cookies. A few times a year she made a carrot ring that served as a vegetable at family dinners, although it had enough Crisco and sugar in it to lubricate and exfoliate a small country.

I have always loved to bake. I love sweets, and baking releases my limited creativity. I like the precise action of measuring the flour into the measuring cup and taking the knife to smooth away the excess. I love cracking eggs and, even better, the challenge of separating the yolks from the whites. How crazy is that? But what I really love is mixing up flavors—sweet milk chocolate with salty nuts or crunching up Oreos into a decadent vanilla cake, which somehow became my famous Oreo cake.

It is the easiest recipe ever, and it was in huge demand in my children's world. Oreo cake became a tradition at most of Rachel and Brian's dearest friends' birthdays or at random celebrations. I even made an Oreo cake to feed a huge crowd at some of the kids' bar mitzvahs. It was elaborately displayed on a mirrored platform so the guests could ooh and aah over it. Really, it was just a simple cake with crushed Oreos mixed into both the batter and the frosting. But to the eater, it was like crack, delivering such a satisfying high that it often became addictive. It made me so happy to make others happy with my silly cake.

My cooking—well, it's not so good. I make things look pretty, but my creativity is challenged, and I don't like following recipes. I have a low tolerance for too many ingredients, too many pots and pans, too many steps in the process, and too many dishes to wash. But during the early days of the pandemic, I stepped up my skills. With my nothing-was-too-much-for-my-family attitude, I stretched my limits and cooked more than ever.

July 2020

In the heat of the summer, Melissa, my daughter Rachel's dear friend since her playgroup days, drove by and dropped off a box of vegetables she bought from one of the local farms near her home. She wanted to support their business, which was struggling due to the pandemic. The virus had spread through the workers, leaving vegetables to die on the plants. We greeted her with smiles behind our masks, took the box with our gloved hands, and eyed the large quantity of green peppers on top of the zucchini. Melissa told us she had made stuffed peppers the night before and shared the recipe in detail. "The zucchini was delicious," she said, "roasted with a touch of sea salt." Rachel and I exchanged a glance, wondering whether we wanted to bring those unwashed vegetables into the house and whether we would eat them.

This was indicative of our corona craziness. We were out of control regarding our food—what we ate, where it came from, and how much we ate. Sweet or salty, it didn't matter—it needed to be clean. That didn't mean a healthy clean where a few germs won't kill you, but super-sanitized like never before. Food had a leading role in our pandemic production, providing comfort, control, connection, consistency—you name it, we needed it.

At the beginning of the journey, we gathered groceries, cleaning supplies, and toilet paper galore. During week one of the shutdown, we subscribed to a grocery delivery service. But after the first three disappointing deliveries—especially the nearly dead romaine lettuce instead of the crisp, super-healthy organic spring mix we'd ordered and the substitution of Spaghetti-Os for quinoa (really?), we knew this wasn't going to work for the controlling food hoarders we were.

Instead, we put on our masks, gloves, and shields and ventured to the supermarket, geared up for the task. After waiting in lines to enter since a limited number of shoppers were allowed in, we purchased items very different from our usual weekly grocery trips. If the shelves were empty, we didn't know what to buy. We just knew that whatever those things were, we needed them.

After we gathered the groceries, we brought them home and usually left the nonperishables outside for several hours so the virus would die before we brought the items into the house. We also washed off those perishable products with Clorox wipes or warm water to kill the virus. We had no idea how to combat this evil COVID, so we took extreme cleaning actions regarding all food products.

The next step was cooking. In the beginning, we cooked every night since we were fearful of takeout food from restaurants. On the rare occasion that we did bring in food, we transferred it outside from the restaurant containers into tin pans and reheated it in our oven to make sure it was COVID-19 free. The experts—also known as our fellow COVID-19-crazy friends—instructed us to reheat the food in a 350-degree oven, and it would be fine. We never brought in raw food such as salads since we didn't trust that the vegetable washing process was as hygienically correct as ours.

With the first cup of morning coffee came the conversation about what we were going to have for dinner. We cooked comfort food from our childhood days (our children's favorites), and we cooked the hip cuisine that our palates had become accustomed to. We cooked "clean" meals (no pun intended) consisting of six items that we humorously named the scruffy bowl. It originally consisted of arugula, tomatoes, avocado, cashews, and sweet potatoes tossed with the juice of a fresh squeezed lime. The scruffy bowl evolved into different variations, but it was "clean." We had themed dinners and breakfast for dinner. There was even a five-day juice cleanse—talk about control. Some unique creations included a giant spaghetti-stuffed meatball, butternut squash soup with coconut milk, and homemade pizza.

"You won't believe what we cooked last night," Laura said to me during our morning Zoom session. "We had gourmet grilled gruyere cheese sandwiches dipped in roasted tomato soup. Can you believe how ridiculous we are?"

Her family, like so many others, came together over food. We cooked together, and we cooked solo, but for the most part a common thread throughout all communities was that cooking was a creative and connecting outlet during a time in our lives when we spent entire days, weeks, and months in our homes.

We learned that siblings bonded while cooking for their families, and they introduced new techniques and tastes. We heard stories of couples creating formal dining atmospheres, including preparing table-side branzino in their one-bedroom, 800-square-foot apartment.

Food was our sustenance and provided pleasure and a great source of entertainment. We cooked with gratitude and love, and the most joyful time of the day was gathering in the evening at the dinner table. Some of us ate with our families or our Quaranteams, and others Zoomed with their loved ones during meals. We dined in socially distanced alfresco fashion with our pods, and there were many who ate alone, meal after meal, relying on the kindness of others to drop off food as an expression of caring during this difficult time.

The art of baking took on a new urgency. Flour, yeast, and sugar were on back order at the grocery stores. People baked bread, pies, cakes, cookies, more bread, and gluten-free everything. While working from home, we were able to let the yeast do its magic and continue the baking process between Zoom meetings. We baked a different cake every Friday and indulged in it over the weekend. The only issue was that we sometimes finished the cake on Friday night, so we baked more all weekend long.

Baking brought fulfillment. By following the recipe, adding just the right ingredients, and baking it for the right amount of time, the finished product—be it a cake, cookies, or chocolate éclair—made us grateful to accomplish something during our days of uncertainty.

My new friend, Spencer, came into our lives the minute I tasted his challah bread that a friend sent to Rachel one Friday for Shabbat. One bite of this yummy decadence and the rest was history. It was dense and delicious.

The following week, Rachel sent one of Spencer's amazing challahs to our house, and I continued to spread the loaves of love to my friends for well wishes or for no reason at all other then I loved supporting "Chollywood Challah" and sharing the COVID-induced creative challah entrepreneur's talent with others. It felt like a way to connect at a time when physical connection was not an option.

Spencer had been living in New York City when he left his office for the last time on a Wednesday in March 2020. A few months later, after he completed his professional contract without a renewal because of COVID, he found himself back in South Florida, living in his parents' home. This is where the challah baking began. First it was just for fun and to eat with his family. Then his creativity kicked in. He began tweaking recipes, receiving positive feedback from his family and friends. He was encouraged to sell his scrumptious challah bread, a traditional food eaten in Jewish homes on Friday nights when celebrating Shabbat (the Sabbath).

The tradition of Shabbat forces us to take a much-needed pause, breaking bread with our families to connect and reflect on the week. These days, challah is a bread enjoyed by everyone. It makes great sandwiches and even better French toast. Spencer's five weekly family challahs quickly grew into a forty-to-sixty-challahs-a-week business with pop-up shops on college campuses in nearby cities. His baking and delivery team included his parents, and they quickly became a BooMillennial business.

"From baking out of my parents' kitchen to branding my product," Spencer shared, "I have learned so much this past year."

Spencer's story is one of many. Cooking became collaborative, and baking was not only delicious but soothing to the soul. We baked for our families, and we gave to others. However, as fortunate as we were to use food for both nutrition and entertainment, many others were struggling with food insecurity. As the economy continued to crumble, the number of individuals experiencing food insecurity during the COVID years grew to record levels. People were hungry, and food banks, homeless shelters, and simple grassroots food collections grew in response. Large refrigerators were strategically placed in some communities where food donations could be dropped off, enabling recipients to anonymously retrieve needed items right out of the community fridge.

Laura and I quickly shifted into full professional mode when a long-time client asked us to connect in the Zoom room for an emergency meeting. Our connector skills were needed in order to fill their food pantry with nonperishable items. "We need your people," the executive director said, knowing that we had an army of generous givers in our portfolio of contacts. "What are your specific needs, time frame, and location of the drop-off?" I asked with a breaking heart in my chest. We had been baking cakes all week while the recipients behind the faces on the Zoom screen needed Saltines and peanut butter to fill the tummies of hungry children.

We got the message and shared it with the masses. One COVID-infected Sunday, dozens and dozens of friends and acquaintances from our Rolodex of givers arrived in the parking lot of our local grocery store, their trunks full of food and essential items. Despite the fact that COVID cases were surging that week in what my dear friend Beth called a "COVID blizzard," we turned out with masks on our faces and weathered the storm, filling the food bank shelves. For us, this was not work; this was who we are and what we do. Especially in times of crisis, our work is not about fees for service; it is about fulfillment, human kindness, and gratitude.

Another up-close-and-personal experience I had with food insecurity began at the crack of dawn one day when I picked up Rachel. Coffee was in the cup holder for her, and we headed forty-five minutes from our home to volunteer at a national organization's food drive to provide food items and essential products for families. Upon arrival, tears swelled in our eyes as we saw the cars lined up as far as we could see.

"Who are these people?" Rachel asked with concern and disbelief, quickly finishing the last few drops of her coffee. Intellectually, she knew who these people were, but it blew her away to see fancy cars filled with people from our neighborhood waiting in line for a chicken, some vegetables, and a box of raisins. Rachel has always been sensitive and compassionate. We reflected for a moment about all the years we had organized Rachel's friends and made hundreds of PB&J sandwiches for the homeless shelter. We remembered the time Rachel tried to give her leftover pancakes from IHOP to a homeless man on the street, and he threw the container back at her. But this was different. We were all living the same nightmare. Why were we the lucky ones? This time the beneficiaries weren't mentally ill or struggling with addiction. They had lost their jobs as a result of COVID-19 and were trying to survive. We shook off our shock, popped a post-coffee breath mint, and got out of the car to begin our work.

Our team of volunteers, including my two dear girlfriends Barbara and Karen, had the highly coveted job of organizing an assembly line to distribute the items into the trunks of the recipients' cars. Great care was taken to uphold the confidentiality and privacy of each of the people pulling into the parking lot. My Millennial daughter Rachel became the logistics manager of the day. At 9:00 a.m., the cars entered the parking lot, and the heavy lifting, both physical and emotional, began.

The cars told the stories of the recipients. These were cars just like we drove—many of them bearing families with two or three children. Prior to COVID-19, they had been living comfortably on two incomes. Now, having lost their jobs due to COVID-19, they were struggling financially and emotionally. Never in their lives did they imagine that their day would begin at dawn waiting in a food distribution line. They had always been the givers, not the recipients.

After we placed the food items into a trunk, we asked the driver if women's sanitary products were needed in their household. We only had a limited supply. One woman was brought to tears as she told us that she had three teenage daughters and was desperate for the items. These people with their trunks open had an unwritten story of pain, embarrassment, uncertainty, and gratitude. It was apparent that for some, their cars had even become their homes. Despite their tired eyes and broken smiles, the deep gratitude was palpable.

And there was much to be grateful for, including being able to grow fruits and vegetables in the Floridian warmth. At the beginning of the pandemic, when grocery store shelves were empty, some began gardening as a means of trying to have some type of control over their own food supply. Others found that with social distancing requirements, gardening provided an outlet, offering the ability to have contact with something real.

"Look what I have for us today," Laura said, holding up two tiny tomatoes. "These are actually from my garden!" she proudly beamed as we sat socially distanced at the table outside on the patio. Laura had never grown anything before, but during the pandemic she found herself in the Home Depot garden section buying seeds, pots, and potting soil to plant a small garden in her backyard. She had been inspired by her sister-in-law, Paula, whose lush organic vegetable garden in Connecticut was producing baskets of fresh vegetables for family, neighbors, and even local nearby restaurants. For many like Paula, gardening became a lifesaver during the height of COVID-19.

While we ate the tomatoes with our favorite working meal—farro salad and PB&J on Dave's bread—Laura shared with me Paula's Instagram of vegetables and flowers. The photo of her dahlias in full bloom put big smiles on our faces.

At a time when we feared losing our health to COVID-19, the overindulgence, deprivation, and everything in between underlined the physical and mental importance of the sustenance we put into our bodies. Laura and I reflected on how important it is to help those who can't help themselves and to appreciate the essential and privileged act of eating. Whether it's a gourmet gruyere grilled cheese or a peanut butter and jelly sandwich, gratitude is the essential ingredient.

6

Hardship and Hope

In Times of Adversity, Work Together to Make Change

June 2020

Laura

/ / I'm leaving," Emily yelled upstairs on a Sunday afternoon. "I'm wearing a mask, and I'll be careful."

"Okay," I said, trying to be calm as she left the house, heading downtown with a few friends to join the protests over the death of George Floyd at the hands of a police officer.

At twenty-two, Emily was an adult, capable of making her own choices. Like many of her contemporaries, she was outraged by police brutality against African Americans. I remember being her age and standing on my Bloomington campus when the Indiana University Student Association adopted a resolution denouncing apartheid in South Africa. Now it was Emily's time. While part of me was stuck in my own spin cycle of neurosis, wondering whether she had remembered to put on sunscreen and take along some water,

I tried to remind myself that she was exactly where she was supposed to be at this moment. She was figuring out what she was passionate about and what she wanted to change in this big, messy world of ours. She was using her voice, advocating for justice, and showing up for what she believed in.

A few years earlier, I took Emily on a civil rights mission. With twenty-five women of varied ages, backgrounds, and levels of social action involvement, we visited Montgomery, Selma, Birmingham, and Atlanta. We toured the Rosa Parks Museum, the Ebenezer Baptist Church, the Edmund Pettus Bridge, and the Equal Justice Initiative. We traced the history of the Black community and learned about the struggle for racial equality. We talked about Emmett Till and studied the words of the heroes who dedicated their lives to demanding justice. Experiencing it with my daughter by my side was incredibly meaningful.

I was born in 1964, the year Martin Luther King Jr. was awarded the Nobel Peace Prize for his nonviolent struggle for African American civil rights. Just four years later, he was assassinated. In 1980, I watched the local Miami news coverage of the riots with the death of Arthur McDuffie. Then in 2020, the world watched on a video loop for nearly nine minutes as a police officer murdered George Floyd. My daughter was entering adulthood at a time of racial injustice and political divide, just as I had and my parents had.

Later that night, as I lay in bed waiting to hear the garage door open, a sign that Emily was home safely, it struck me that despite all the changes our country has witnessed over the many decades, so much has stayed the same. As parents, we are constantly navigating the need to keep our children safe but at the same time encouraging them to show up and speak up for what matters. We toss and turn and wrestle with worry. Did we prepare them for the world that awaits them?

In the summer of 2020, the world felt like it was in chaos. My life felt like it was at a standstill, but I was unable to sit still. With our adult children living in our homes, Adrian and I were keenly aware that we needed to step up—we needed to *do* something. So we began to do what we do best—convene people. This time it was not in person but remotely. We connected with people in other cities and in our Miami community and heard incredible stories of ordinary people doing extraordinary things. Nurses and doctors were working tirelessly day after day taking care of patients in hospitals and comforting their families. Teachers were showing patience and resourcefulness in the most innovative ways. Parents were figuring out how to become resident teachers, short-order chefs, and technology troubleshooters.

COVID-19 derailed our world. Yet through the hardships, there was hope on the horizon. People became more understanding and empathetic. They expressed a collective generosity as they came together to volunteer, donate time and money, and support friends, family, and neighbors. They sang on balconies, lined the streets to applaud healthcare workers, and distributed food to those in need. They repurposed and donated iPads so patients in hospitals could communicate with their family members. They baked and delivered snacks to local frontline healthcare workers to show gratitude for their dedication during this time. There was kindness and a tremendous commitment to community. People rose to the challenge with vision and fortitude, bringing out the very best of themselves when it was most needed.

When COVID-19 hit, our nonprofit world changed. The old way of doing business as usual was no longer relevant. Organizations quickly got up to speed, organizing digital fundraisers to continue to steward supporters and donors and planning virtual fundraisers with clever cocktails and food delivered to guests' homes. In the nonprofit world, new businesses popped up, stepping in to elevate at-home fundraising events and provide entertainment right from someone's kitchen table or living room sofa.

Creative collaboration, good leadership, and personal follow-up became the vehicles for success. Decisions had to be made, and Zoom technology was the method for convening. Many organizations needed to quickly become educated on how to deliver online programs while continuing to do business and maintaining their staff and donor base.

Adrian and I worked with one of our clients to pivot her annual face-to-face fundraiser efforts into the Zoom room space. It allowed her to share the message of her mission to people she had never reached before. An online platform that let everyone engage, become educated, and ultimately give turned out to be a win-win business model, one that continues after the COVID era.

Mary, a colleague of mine and an associate development director for a nonprofit organization in Miami, shared that "2020 was a lesson in learning to adapt in real time."

Many who have experienced virtual fundraisers now say they prefer not having to get dressed up and sit at a traditional gala for an entire evening. Others still want fundraisers to be in person. During COVID, we saw a lot of financial generosity with overall giving levels increasing by more than five percent. Organizations figured out how to adapt, continue to utilize their volunteers, and serve their missions.

Large nonprofit organizations such as the Red Cross, Goodwill, and others came through, showing collaboration and generosity to meet the needs of this time. The Jewish Federations of North America leveraged their network of 146 local chapters throughout North America, Israel, and around the world to identify, support, and address the full range of social service issues and provide life-saving humanitarian relief. At this critical time when so many were in need, people stepped up. Our organizations could not fail; too many people were counting on them.

"If you're grateful, say it out loud, and that will multiply." These inspiring words are from Gaby, the executive director of a nonprofit that started out as a small community service project and is now a well-established diaper bank in Miami. Gaby first became aware of the need for diaper distribution when she was the young mom of her son. The organization's mission was to collect and distribute diapers and other related products to families in need while also raising awareness about the need for diaper donations. She so believed in the mission of the organization that she got involved in planning collections and distributions and helping strategize how to scale up the organization.

Since diapers are not eligible for federally subsidized food stamps or WIC (Women, Infants, and Children—a special supplemental nutrition program), the cost of diapers puts an enormous financial strain on struggling families just trying to make ends meet. It's nearly impossible for many families to afford enough clean diapers for their children without the help of organizations such as the Miami Diaper Bank. It's reported that one in three American families must choose between diapers and other basic needs such as food.

With an outgoing personality, attention to detail, follow-through, and excellent social media know-how, Gaby was able to raise awareness, increase partnerships, and help grow the budget of the organization exponentially from what it was when she first began working with them in 2017. She got teary with pride when she reflected on her professional growth. "Let me pause as I say this out loud. Tomorrow I am going to my first grants lunch meeting!" she said with elation. "I feel so fortunate to be able to serve others." Adrian and I felt equally fortunate to witness Gaby's growth and the organization's success.

Despite these positive stories, there was a feeling of help-lessness and hopelessness that permeated our country during COVID. One day I was speaking with my friend Robyn, a rabbi and spiritual leader who is beloved in her community. I listened as she fleshed out her upcoming sermon. "This is our time to recalibrate our world and to reinstate economic justice into our society and environmental justice onto the planet," she read aloud to me.

It was true that yes, we were all experiencing the pandemic together, but each of us was experiencing it very differently. Race, socioeconomic status, age, and where you live had a dramatic impact on everyone's personal situation. While I worried about my parents staying healthy, my mother-in-law feeling isolated, and my kids' working lives being upended, I knew so many others who had lost family, friends, jobs or even entire businesses. Across all demographics, we saw an increase in mental illness, anxiety, and substance abuse. And for all of us, our sense of security was lost.

The sadness and suffering of this time also brought tre-mendous awareness. Images of children separated from their parents at the US border—parents who had risked every-thing for a better life—fully exposed the complexities of the immigration policy. Mass shootings with far too much senseless loss continued to keep the issue of gun control at the forefront.

Widening the economic gap in education, the pandemic brought the inequities of our educational system to the surface.

Student success varied widely, depending on geographic location and economic status. For vulnerable students, this time was extremely challenging. Online schooling meant a decline in grades and frustration for many parents whose children experienced a lack of instruction as well as difficulty with technological issues and access to the Internet. It became clear that in most cases, students learn most effectively in person in a traditional classroom with a teacher, peers, and activities.

Ben, my friend Julie's son, began his teaching career straight out of college, joining Teach for America and thinking he would stay just long enough to finish the two-year service commitment. In 2020, he had been a special education teacher with the New York Public School System for more than eight years. As a teacher in the Bronx, he became invested in the school and the surrounding community.

"There's a reason I'm still here," he said. "I believe in the mission." As the team leader for the school's sixth grade and head of the math department, he wears many hats at the school. Ben said that when the COVID lockdown began, the school was in no way set up to teach a remote program. They were grateful and fortunate that they were able to locate all their students, but they had a tremendous amount of work to do to deliver an educational program of any caliber to them. Just like the rest of the world, the teachers and administration were facing their own personal real-life challenges, and some of the staff returned to their hometowns to shelter in place.

I met Ben's mom, Julie, when our sons were in Mommy and Me. Over the decades, we shared milestones in our children's lives and marveled at their growth. Early in the summer of 2020, Ben put his dog in the car and drove from New York to Miami to quarantine with his family. His two younger brothers also came home. Ben said it was certainly humorous teaching virtually from his childhood bedroom. One of his brothers took virtual college classes on Zoom. The other brother, an attorney, attended online hearings from his bedroom down the hall.

Ben said that in addition to the pandemic, racial tension added another layer of challenge to the school year. Having been in his position for many years, this was not new to him, but now he was compelled to reexamine his role as a teacher and administrator, shaping policy for the school and acting as a mentor to his students. Ben said, "I've really had to ask myself, 'What is my place in this, and what can I do to have the most impact?' It's been a time when I'm asking myself, 'What kind of leader do I want to be?'"

In addition to the disruption of classroom learning, the loss of after-school activities and sports also had a profound effect on students' education. Not only were students relegated to their computer screens for most of their school day, but now they no longer had a creative or athletic outlet or the opportunity to get together with friends and teammates, something that had been a staple of students' physical and social development in the past.

A Temple youth basketball league in Miami has been connecting diverse communities for more than forty-five years. Many kids would tell you that what they remember most about the league is that everyone who tries out makes the team, and everyone gets the same amount of playing time, no matter what. Although some kids do excel at basketball and some over-testosteroned fathers may bring an intensity to the sidelines, the league's focus is not actually about being skilled at basketball. It is about appreciating everyone's talents and learning to work together for the good of the team. The league drew attention from local professional players who mentored kids over the years and put their own young kids in the league because it exemplified the best of what playing sports can teach us.

Danny is a product of this synagogue's basketball league. Like many men, Danny said he marked the start of the pandemic—"the day I knew it was real"—when the NBA canceled its season. "I just couldn't believe it," he told us.

Danny worked as a writer-producer in the television industry, including the popular show *Blackish*. He is one of "our" kids. We are deeply proud of him and look to him as one of the next generation's game-changers. Danny's mother, Lisa, was the synagogue's cantor for twenty years, and his father is a third-generation Miamian. Danny sees himself as a storyteller, and he's constantly asking himself how he can best tell a story.

Danny said he learned how to ask questions by attending Temple events. "I know how to speak to white, middle-aged women," he said jokingly. "Growing up as a cantor's son gave me the ability to schmooze and ask questions."

Danny is humble and says he loves what he does. He sees his role as a gift—to be perfectly placed at a time and place where he can create bridges between communities and bring understanding to the issues. Early in the pandemic, he was able to help Black people tell their stories and promote diverse new voices, specifically from the African American community, which is more important than ever.

Always a funny and outgoing kid, Danny says humor gives people the ability to learn and find understanding—to unpack misconceptions and become more aware. He says there's no replacement for individual conversation and that his learning curve on a day-to-day basis was "massive."

"Morale is high," he said with a big, optimistic grin. "I'm grateful and humbled to be in this time and to have this space to help share these stories."

COVID-19 undeniably exposed the inequities in the world and accentuated the differences between the haves and the have-nots. Americans have also experienced the full display of cancel culture where anyone can publicly "call out" or "cancel" anyone else for anything they don't agree with. It shows how inflammatory and intolerant we have become as a society, indicating a broader problem in our world—our need as individuals to be comfortable and validated in our own opinions and beliefs. When did we abandon open-minded discussion and the ability to agree to disagree? When did we lose confidence in our ability to work together?

In 2020, we lost two of our country's most courageous and inspirational leaders—Ruth Bader Ginsberg, whose legacy of pursuing justice, especially for women's rights, will live on and inspire future generations of women and girls; and John Lewis who taught us what it means to stand up against all odds and fight for what you believe in and what you know is right, even if it means getting in "good trouble." And oh, how I miss level-headed leaders such as Senator John McCain and Senator Bob Dole.

In the height of the pandemic, we witnessed so much hardship, and yet we learned new ways to adapt, collaborate, and work together. In this moment in history when the world was on hold, we each had an opportunity to look within, reevaluate our purpose, and gain perspective on what really matters. Hopefully, we will remember what we accomplished and use what we have learned throughout the pandemic to create a stronger, more equitable country where there is opportunity for all. It is up to each of us to be informed, continue to educate ourselves, and shine our light where there is darkness.

We are constantly reminded of the importance of adding value where we can. Whether it's an organization or a group of volunteers collecting for a cause, a team, or a family, each of us can contribute something. This period of time has shown us that when we work together, keeping hope in our hearts, what we can accomplish is infinite.

7

Loss and Loneliness

In Tough Times, Be Sensitive and Kind

July 2020

Adrian

With a heavy heart and a box of tissues, I watched *60 Minutes* on CBS as journalist Scott Pelley interviewed several families who had lost loved ones to COVID-19. Many of the bereaved found the loss of loved ones surreal. People of all ages, races, and religions lost their lives, and family members lost their loved ones. As Pelley said, "When a parent dies too young, children age too soon." These powerful words describe many children who were left with only one parent or who tragically lost both parents to COVID-19. They became orphans.

There were stories of couples both young and old saying goodbye at the hospital emergency room door and never seeing one another in person again. Their last conversations took place via Facetime or a phone call. People in the hospital were alone and dying, and their loved ones outside the hospital were alone and isolated. In some cases, family members were not able to gather for the traditional funeral and interment, leading to a lack of closure.

I spoke to a few people who had the painful experience of not being able to travel to see their dying loved ones or attend their burials. At my annual checkup, my doctor, whose mother died during the pandemic, described it as "psychologically unsettling." Unable to envision her deceased family member, she was left with no closure and tremendous pain "like an open wound on my heart forever."

The pandemic created deep loss and loneliness, with death being just one of many strains of loss as a result of COVID-19. People lost people both literally and figuratively, leading to a condition in our world known as the "loneliness epidemic."

Loneliness has been a concern in the mental health sphere for decades, most recently with a focus on the aging senior population. Loneliness can be defined as the space between the social connections an individual would like to have and the reality of their social interaction experience.

When I was growing up, most of my extended family lived within a five-mile radius of each other, allowing for family interactions both planned and impromptu. It was easy to call my grandma, aunts, uncles, and cousins and ask them if they wanted to run errands with me, come over for a cookout, or share some of my mom's famous chili on a cold, winter night. We could plan, prepare, and provide companionship easily. It was inherent behavior where almost daily connection and communication with aging family members was our way of life. My generation grew up and often left their hometowns. Thanks to modern medicine and healthier lifestyles, the senior population began living longer, more active, and independent lives, igniting the desire for communal senior and super senior living facilities. Communal living for seniors became very popular, allowing the maturing and geriatric needs of this generation to be served while also promoting their connection with others of the same age.

My friend Leslie shared the story of her father who died at ninety-five, not directly from COVID-19 but from collateral damage from the virus. He spent his final years in an assisted-living facility due to his failing health, and his emotional wounds as a Holocaust survivor prevented him from connecting with others, even his daughter. He was strong-willed and independent, a true survivor who did not want to need anyone. At ninety-two, he was finally able to break out of his emotional isolation and hesitantly accept the help of others. He never knew how much he had missed by being emotionally closed off until he released and let the love flow. Leslie refers to this time as when the love story began with her father. Although he died during lockdown, he died a bit less lonely, filled with the love he had rarely enjoyed.

I've known Leslie for more than twenty years since we both have a seat in our mutually adored stock club. We have had many conversations regarding our work, our families, and the financial world. I attended her mother's funeral several years ago, and we celebrated memories of the fun times we'd had together at our stock club gatherings and even a funky spa day. But I never knew the story of her father's life. Shortly after he passed away, Leslie, Laura, and I met in the Zoom room and shared tears together when we heard details of her father's life as a Holocaust survivor.

There are many stories of Holocaust survivors who experienced loneliness throughout their lives. The loss of their families in concentration camps left them with unmendable holes in their hearts—gaps in their lives that affected their relationships with friends, family, and even food. Family relationships of these survivors have been studied for decades, with a focus on their "survivor baggage," including weak emotional connectivity and strong control issues. The living survivors are now "super seniors" who quite often live alone. Their suppressed loneliness often rises to the surface as they age and as they spend most of their time alone with their own thoughts day in and day out.

After many grueling months of the pandemic, I finally connected with our longtime friend Lisa via Zoom. With both exhaustion and exhilaration, she brought this sad reality to life when she shared the work of an organization she volunteers for that provides a lifeline to the elderly, including many Holocaust survivors. Once lockdowns began, joyful senior living stopped, and the usual quick flight to visit mom or dad came to a halt. Lisa felt how deeply the senior population in her life was being adversely affected. There was no one to eat with or share a card game with. There was no one to give or receive a hug. Everyone needs to be touched, and hugs are medicine to most, especially the elderly population.

In a touch-free world, Lisa touched many lonely lives with great authenticity and love. She provided warmth and connection to Avram, an 88-year-old Ukrainian man who lived alone, his family unable to travel to care for him. Her special elderly ladies were Rachel and Rose. She called them every day and when possible brought them food and essential items. She organized a Zoom call for Rachel and her family, allowing them to virtually celebrate Rachel's birthday. Being able to "be there" for these women and their families and providing them with comfort and elevating their spirits during the loneliest of times gave Lisa fulfillment and a sense of purpose during those dark days. She had been volunteering and serving the senior community for many years, but COVID-19 elevated her work to a new level.

During this time of disconnection, technology was both a blessing and a curse to the senior community. Some of the savvier seniors brought themselves into the world of Zoom and Facetime, which allowed them to stay in touch with loved ones. But for the majority of this population, it was difficult, both technically and financially.

As real as the digital divide is with the senior community, one would think that technology would help younger generations such as Millennials and Gen Z-ers stay connected and avoid loneliness. But according to Dr. Richard Weissbourd, psychologist and senior lecturer at the Harvard Graduate School of Education, rates of loneliness among young people are surprisingly high.

My sorority sister's Millennial daughter Nicole spent three of her four semesters of graduate school living the pandemic lifestyle. She shared that "the fear of the virus, isolation, virtual learning, and friends with mixed beliefs regarding mask-wearing and social distancing all prompted my ongoing battle with anxiety to go up while my self-esteem and happiness went straight down." At age twenty-six and living alone with no social or physical outlet other than technology and social media, Nicole found herself facing a dark rabbit hole of panic attacks, depression, and loneliness.

Without family nearby or the ability to travel, Nicole began self-medicating and stopped functioning at the level her coursework required. Fortunately, the university identified her struggle, and she received mental health counseling. Nicole was shocked at how quickly her well-planned, structured, and highly productive life shifted out of control. She had always had reinforcement from the people in her life. Without people, she crumbled, lost in her loneliness and circling thoughts.

Several years ago, Good Work Miami hosted an event at a local bookstore for our friend and author Debra Fine to introduce her book *Beyond Texting: The Fine Art of Face-to-Face Communication for Teenagers*. The book was for both teens and their parents, teaching them how to be appropriately "plugged in" without neglecting the power of physical human interaction. One of the reasons we felt it was so important to help Debra get her message out was because I was so traumatized by my own children's texting behavior during their teenage years. I was still looking for validity regarding my feelings about the importance of face-to-face communication and human connection.

When Rachel was fifteen years old and the fancy flip phone came out with texting capabilities, I vividly remember how lost I felt in my parenting role. One of my favorite places to spend time with my kids was in the car driving them to and from school and all of their various activities in their pre-driving years. We would talk about our day, sing along with the radio, and have a great time communicating and connecting. When the fancy flip phone came, the mother-daughter drama began.

"What are you doing on your phone?" I asked with both curiosity and sadness.

"One minute, Mom," she said as her fingers magically typed sentiments to her friends, leaving me out of the conversation.

I seethed. This was our time. I wanted her attention. How dare she text her friends during our precious car time together? I had not yet learned to text or at least not with her lightning speed. What was she saying to her friends in their secret space? Why couldn't she just say the words out loud into the phone so I could eavesdrop in typical parenting style? She was very focused on communicating with her peeps, and in my hurt feelings I felt left out and frightened at times. I even remember crying during one of our car rides because Rachel was totally disconnected from me and completely connected to the keypad on her phone. What a huge shift.

My sweet son Brian even broke up with his first girlfriend via text. After spending the summer apart while he was at sleepaway camp and she was home counting the days until his return, he ended their teen romance with a text. Really? How quickly he moved on from what seemed to me like an insensitive act, and how quickly I learned that texting was here to stay and that the definition of communication, connecting, and talking had changed. Even now, Brian tells me he has been "talking" to someone, and when I drill down with my usual questions, "talking" means texting. The years have brought us beyond texting into the world of social media and advanced technology, bearing the good, the bad, and everything in between.

During the pandemic, I heard many stories of FOMO— fear of missing out—induced by anxiety and leading to increased loneliness. The definition of FOMO shifted as the lockdown came into effect. It gave rise to a vicious fear of missing out on all we hoped would be taking place in our lives—the fear that the canceled concert we had tickets for would never be rescheduled or that the wedding we'd planned would not happen. FOMO became hyper-apparent in the virtual world with great negative effects on all generations but especially on younger folks who are social media obsessed in the best of times. This obsession became even more magnified during the crazy coronavirus times.

FOMO comes from the human need to compare ourselves to others. It can lead to depression and loneliness while skewing a sense of gratitude and mindfulness. Pandemic FOMO was different. Instead of focusing on where people were vacationing or partying, locked-down people had FOMO looking at a smiling family baking sourdough bread together. The result was the same—feelings of anxiety, sadness, and deep loneliness.

My daughter Rachel's lifelong friend Jolie, a Millennial physician in New York City, shifted to a frontline, life-saving hospital professional overnight when the coronavirus landed in the city. She worked brutal hours, fully donned in personal protective equipment (PPE) as she admitted, examined, and intubated patients day after day, week after week. Both Jolie and her fiancé fell ill with COVID-19 in mid-March 2020. Her family supported her emotionally from a distance. The feeling of isolation, exhaustion, and despair even led her to rethink her profession as a physician, a career she had worked very hard to acquire.

"In a sea of sickness, I felt a sense of uncertainty and loneliness like never before," Jolie told me. "As I worked to save lives, I felt as if I were losing myself and was desperate for the strength and support of my loved ones."

I'm so proud of Jolie, the little girl who grew up playing in my house and then became an accomplished and empathetic young woman and accomplished doctor.

Loneliness surfaced in lives across generations, demographics, and personal situations.

My friend Annette, a widow with two young adult children, lost her husband almost a decade ago. Her loneliness stems from missing her parenting partner. She called him "the other person who would truly feel the accomplishment and joy when my son was accepted into medical school and when my daughter virtually graduated from college last spring." She also shared, "My kids were extremely fearful of me getting COVID-19 and possibly dying. I think this comes from them losing their father and not wanting to be orphans."

The fragility of both our physical and mental health has been tested during this time of loss and loneliness. Due to COVID-19, we have endured the tragedy of death, collateral damage to our health, anxiety, depression, suicide, and the pain of being alone. We have acquired a heightened awareness of other people's situations and struggles, recognizing the importance of taking time to chat with an elderly person who is starved for conversation or listen to a grieving person who has a story to share about their lost loved one.

We've realized how crucial it is to connect with the young adult who is struggling with demons in their mind, the recent college graduate who feels lost and alone trying to move forward while many pathways are closed, and the most vulnerable who are alone on the streets of life. Even technology, which I once found to be a great disrupter, was both a culprit and a connector. Loss and loneliness, the great trauma of this time, can only be remedied by human connection. People need people during the good times, bad times, and everything in between.

8

Realigning Relationships

Honor the Relationships That Matter Most

August 2020

Laura

The COVID period tested people's relationships. Since we were no longer attending in-person sporting events, concerts, or celebrations, the pandemic reconfigured people's social interactions to our quarantine mates or those we could visit with on screen. There was no planning, no parties, and no special occasions on the calendar. For my husband Dan and me, riding out the pandemic together brought to mind that old adage—"Married for life but not for lunch." Together day after day, hour after hour, my husband and I began to feel as if we were starring in our own sitcom, and it wasn't much of a comedy. No matter how happy, considerate, flexible, or easygoing we were, nothing quite prepared us for a global pandemic. Nothing! When they give the whole "for better, for worse, in sickness and in health" speech, nowhere in there did it ever mention "and in a global pandemic."

"Just extract yourself from the situation," my sister Julie said to me. In the many months of quarantine, with four of us working virtually from the house, I went to the back of Dan's closet if I really needed to have a private conversation. There, settled amidst the shirt sleeves wafting with the subtle hint of his cologne, I was far away from any of the faint reverberations of various voices on Zoom. His closet was my oasis, my peaceful retreat from the reality TV show that my real life had become. Seated on the floor with the dog at my feet, I made phone calls, answered emails, had a cup of coffee or a snack, and eventually called my sisters to catch up and hear about their day.

"I am literally sitting in Dan's closet," I said, "because there is nowhere else to hear myself think."

Laughing, listening, complaining, or crying, my sisters and I usually spoke every afternoon. I made them laugh about the lunacy playing out in my house, and they shared their perspectives. My sister Karen's son and daughter were also home in their Boca Raton home, sharing shifting workspaces, enjoying beautiful weather, and cooking ridiculously elaborate meals each night. My other sister Julie lived in Dallas, far away from her three sons who were all in their twenties and scattered in three different cities, unable to travel home.

It was either too much togetherness or too much isolation and loneliness. No arrangement was ideal.

"Couples learned a lot about each other in lockdown," my friend Helen observed. An attorney and mediator who provided mediation to divorcing couples, Helen shared how she and her colleagues noticed that many people were "overwhelmed and anxious. When there's heightened anxiety, that's when people reach out for legal help."

Helen's son Justin had grown up with my Andrew and Adrian's son Brian. Helen was always a level-headed parent and friend, and I appreciated her perspective. Professionally, Helen had a mission to change the way divorce was experienced and eliminate the need for the court's involvement. She highlighted the difficulty of couples who had to work through their issues with their young children at home with them. For months when Helen spoke to people during the lockdown, she said, "It was sad to hear them huddled outside over a phone so their child couldn't hear." Through Facetime, she saw the worry and frustration of parents trying to work through issues and figure out what was best for their families without the necessary space to have open and honest conversations.

For some people, being confined together made their relationship stronger. Some couples thrived during this time, drawing strength from one another and grateful to have a partner to lean on and a strong relationship to support them. Even if it was just a warm body sitting nearby while streaming mindless TV shows or processing the day's news, having a companion in this vulnerable time was appreciated.

For the months of lockdown, it seemed there was no end to content that vied for people's attention. A slew of innovative new programming was quickly developed, and in an effort to feel connected, I logged onto to almost everything. I listened to authors talk about their books along with economists and political pundits pontificating on the current state of our country. Some days, my son Jacob and his wife Steph came over after work, and Steph and I would cook dinner while watching an online program with Carolyn, a Canadian chef who Steph's brother knew. From her kitchen in Montreal, Carolyn sliced, diced, prepped, and prepared delicious meals in under an hour, passing along her tricks of the trade to a weekly online audience of devoted disciples.

I logged on to endless webinars and conversations on a multitude of topics. From taking a virtual tour of *Downton Abbey* to learning about the history of the Fabergé eggs and Impressionist painting, there was no end to the offerings. Dan and I listened to art talks and logged on with friends for virtual wine tastings. Emily and I took virtual mindfulness classes where we tried desperately to "sit in our stillness and quiet our minds."

There were book clubs and stock clubs that switched their monthly get-togethers to online. Bridge games and mahjong games moved to online platforms, connecting friends from around the world. Pre-pandemic, my father's group of friends, the (ROMEOS (Retired Old Men Eating Out) gathered for lunch to discuss everything from politics, prostates, and their most recent round of golf. They, too, learned to tackle technology and logged on to their computers every week to share the same lively conversations and connect.

I listened to Martha Stewart give an online demonstration on cake decorating and Katie Couric and Ina Garten chuckling over cocktails on Zoom as they chatted about comfort food. Beloved talk show host Phil Donahue and his wife, Marlo Thomas, got personal with their new book *What Makes a Marriage Last*. Couples brought their wit, wisdom, and honesty right into people's homes. How about *That Girl*? The creativity and resourcefulness of this time was astonishing.

Back in the '70s, there weren't as many choices. Most people were doing the same thing. In the late afternoon, kids were outside playing with other kids in their neighborhoods or watching a half-hour TV show while moms made dinner and dads commuted home from work. Today, no one is doing the same thing. You can stream any show you want at any time. You can stop it, start it, and save it to watch later. You can have multiple screens on at the same time or log in, turn your camera off, and pay attention to nothing. Yet ironically, with all the advances and conveniences of our modern, connected world, what has been lost is our cultural connections. In all the customization, we've lost the commonality of what it's like to experience the same thing at the same time. But the online platforms did help us create new ways to bring the generations together.

In the first weeks of the pandemic, I was very worried about my parents. I worried about them staying healthy and safe, and I worried about my dad becoming frustrated that he could not see his family. At 84, he is probably the most optimistic, high-energy, positive person I know. As the patriarch of our family, he's an extremely hardworking and generous man, grateful for his many blessings and valuing more than anything else family and being together. And I mean *together*—like *My Big Fat Greek* (in this case, Jewish) *Wedding* togetherness.

My father's parents came to the United States in 1913. My grandmother was born in Russia and my grandfather in Austria. Like most immigrants, their story was one of courage and perseverance. They came to the United States hoping for freedom, enduring all kinds of hardships for the promise of a better life. My sisters and I grew up hearing my father's stories of his childhood in a small town in the Catskill Mountains. He was the youngest of three boys, all who worked long hours in the family mattress business.

At age fourteen, when my dad's older brothers were off serving in the Army, Dad was out driving the old pickup truck making deliveries throughout upstate New York. With an exemplary work ethic and the help of his high school principal and basketball coach, he received a full scholarship to the University of Michigan—and the opportunity to escape his small town to create a bigger life for himself.

Like many in his generation, my dad continued to move ahead. He was fortunate to encounter people along his path who helped him in small but profound ways. To this day, he takes every opportunity to share his stories of how one person can make a difference and change someone's life. He is my role model for how to live a life of integrity, generosity, and purpose. And to my father, family is everything.

So one Friday evening, amidst the quarantine haze while we were busy hoarding toilet paper like the rest of the world, we planned a family Zoom call. There were seventeen family members in total—my parents (both in their eighties), my sisters and me, our husbands, and nine grandchildren ranging in age from twenty-one to twenty-nine and spread across the country from California to New York. Each of us had our faces in different boxes on the screen. It was a welcome opportunity to take a break, share a laugh, and update each other on the small or large events of the week. It quickly became a weekly tradition, something to give structure to our world that seemed to be spinning out of control. Some weeks were more animated than others, and some weeks were just a blur of the week before—a peppering of questions such as "What are you making for dinner?" and "What are you watching on TV?"

Some weeks not everyone was able to join, and some weeks the political discussions were a bit too much. My sister Karen recalled one Friday in September when she unmuted herself and said, "Dad, if you say one word about the election, I'm getting off this call!" No one in the family could imagine that fifty-two weeks later we would still be logging on every

Friday night. But undoubtedly, the Friday night family Zoom ritual gave cadence to our lives and will be one of the most profound memories to come out of this time. While nothing can take the place of being together in person, we've learned how to use technology to keep us connected.

Now more than ever, our relationships mean everything, and we don't take them for granted. Amidst the chaos of the pandemic, I, like many, relied on my family and friends to pull me through that time of uncertainty. The "Zroom," as it affectionately became known among our friends, made it possible for us to be together. I remember when my friend Tracey set up the very first of what became for a while a weekly tradition—a Zoom girls' happy hour. Five of our friends all logged on with cocktails at 5:00 p.m. None of us had seen each other since the start of the pandemic. Like the opening of *The Brady Bunch*, we were ecstatic at the joy of being able to see each other's faces and laugh with glasses of Sauvignon Blanc in hand. Always creative, Tracey led us through an opening ice breaker, and within a few minutes and another glass of wine, we talked and talked, sharing information and processing the unknown together.

Soon, however, the novelty wore off. As days and weeks passed, it wasn't the peripheral people in my life I wanted to spend my energy on. Instead, I really wanted to connect with my old friends. Wendy and I had been friends since our boys were in preschool. In this time of such seriousness and uncertainty, our friendship morphed into weekly walking dates. We laughed and marveled over the fact that somehow she and her ex-husband and his girlfriend found themselves forming a family dinner pod, gathering every Sunday. They planned a weekly menu and assigned recipes, and everyone came together each week to share a meal and forge a path together to combat the loneliness of the pandemic.

Wendy recounted that although this time was difficult as a single person, she adapted and thrived, becoming more connected to herself and devoting time to raising her awareness of important issues. She joined a women's group that met online weekly to learn about racial inequality. In educating herself on the history of injustice, inequity, racism, and prejudice, she found her sense of purpose. She appreciated having the space to be vulnerable, process difficult concepts, and build friendships with women.

Many of my friends found or rediscovered the joy of stillness and solitude. They found they no longer desired some friendships the way they once had, pre-pandemic. It is not easy to change the rules of the game on friendship patterns determined long ago. Finding a new comfortable cruising altitude in an old friendship takes time and can often feel uncomfortable. Over the years, while some friendships may fade into the background or fall off completely, other friendships deepen and grow. For Baby Boomers, many adult friendships formed decades ago while their children were growing up. As moms, they sat on the bleachers, rotating through the seasons of Little League and ballet recitals. They cherish these shared experiences and see how those friendships have nurtured their children. These old friends have known each other's children and been part of their entire lives.

Throughout the pandemic, I, like many, clung to my closest friends but let go of some of the more peripheral friendships in my life. I continued to value what Stanford sociologist Mark Granovetter calls "weak ties," referring to the importance of people and acquaintances we see infrequently and don't know well. According to Granovetter, our weak-tie connections tether us to the world at large, keeping us from isolating ourselves within networks of people who are the same as we are and challenge us and help us grow.

During COVID, most people were forced to live a more homogeneous existence than ever before. There was a greater appreciation for the acquaintances in our day-to-day routine—the front desk guy at the gym, the Starbucks barista who knew our coffee preferences, and the people who recognized us at our favorite restaurant. Psychiatrist Robert Waldinger, who conducted a study at Harvard, concluded that the key to life's overall happiness is the quality of our relationships. It is not necessary to have dozens of friends. What matters is having a wide range of "weak ties" and a handful of deep relationships with people who really have our backs.

My mother-in-law, Judi, was one of the many people who lost loved ones in the pandemic. Bob, the second great love of her life, passed away at almost 92 years old, and she was brokenhearted. While her whole family was concerned about her feeling lonely and isolated, her best friend, Marcia, helped her heal and move forward. They are as close as sisters, both women say. It was their standing five o'clock phone call—"C and C" (cocktail and conversation)—that sustained them throughout the pandemic.

My mother-in-law lives in a historic colonial house in beautiful Westport, Connecticut, an easy train ride from New York City. She has always enjoyed coming to the city for lunches, dinners, theater, opera, and walks through museums. When the world changed in early 2020, Judi and Marcia adapted, and as with most friendships that are sturdy enough to withstand decades, these true friends found a way to be there for one another, no matter the distance or masking requirements. Their "daily debrief" during lockdown evolved organically. Every day they touched base and processed the enormity of everything going on in the world. They recapped the news or just shared stories about their grandchildren.

Some days their talks were so deep that they were in tears. These were trying times, and the issues both in their personal lives and the world at large were real and raw. Both were strong women with a lot of life experience, so they were well-versed in dealing with the hurdles that life had presented them. Ups and downs, tremendous joys, and devastating losses, both women developed through faith and friendship the fortitude to forge ahead. They were resilient and optimistic that life has a way of working out.

The COVID time made us grateful for our friendships and brought clarity to who we could count on in our lives. One Thursday in May, I got in the car and drove across the Sunny Isles causeway. I pulled into the parking lot that was the midway meeting place where my friend Lisie and I usually meet when she came down to Florida to visit her parents. It was usually impossible to find a spot in the parking lot, but on that day, there was hardly anyone there due to COVID.

Standing on the sidewalk was a woman looking down at her phone, barely recognizable behind her sunglasses. She had a pink baseball hat on and a mask covering her face. But I would know Lisie anywhere. We joke that we met in utero. Our mothers were best friends, our fathers grew up together in New York, and growing up as kids, we lived three houses away from each other until we both left for college. After we graduated, we were roommates in New York City, sharing an apartment on West 62nd Street during the mid-1980s, the era of big hair and big shoulder pads.

Three weeks into my single-in-the-big-city sojourn with my roommate by my side, I met the man I would marry a year and a half later.

"Is he like *balding* balding?" I asked Lisie after Dan walked me back to the apartment on the night we first met.

"Yes, he is *balding* balding," she said, "but he's really cute." The following week, Dan sent me flowers on the first day of my new job, an entry-level position at a large advertising agency. A few weeks later, we met each other's parents, and just four months later, like one of those whirlwind New York City stories, we got engaged at the skating rink at Rockefeller Center. To say that we didn't overthink it is an understatement—we were just two young fools who found each other. Probably as shell-shocked as I was, Lisie generously welcomed *Dano*, his bike, and all of his 24-year-old belongings into our apartment and our life. Almost a decade later, I walked down the aisle as Lisie's maid of honor when she married Michael. And here we were, decades later in the spring of 2020, meeting for lunch at a strip mall. Lisie was the first person I knew who was brave enough to get on a plane and fly from her home in Maryland to Miami, anxious to check on her mother who had not been feeling well.

Although it felt like forever, it had only been three months since we last saw each other. That was before the world changed. I parked and got out of my car, and we ran to meet each other. With both hands, we grabbed each other's wrists, holding on tight as tears welled in our eyes behind our sunglasses and masks. We couldn't hug. This was insanity.

"I brought you a salad," I said to her as we set up our makeshift lunch on an outdoor bench. I took out two plastic containers of greens, some water, utensils, and a bottle of hand sanitizer. We talked about everything and nothing, grateful just to be able to sit together in person. There was an unmistakable, steady undercurrent of anxiety to our conversation. We were nervous about our aging parents, nervous about the virus, and nervous about our children.

"We need to practice self-care," she said, "or so they tell me." We were learning to live our lives with very few answers and little control.

Self-care came in different forms during the pandemic. For me, it was in the form of a thirty-seven-pound Goldendoodle named Louie. This little love of my life became my total obsession. He roamed from room to room in our house, made his rounds, and checked on "his" people. Sitting in his usual spot at my feet, he might have been a bit flustered in the early days of the pandemic. After all, trying to distinguish between in-person voices and Zoom voices was sometimes complicated even for humans. Eventually, he learned to adapt, and barking dogs in backgrounds on computer screens became one of the most familiar and often heartwarming images of the time, adding warmth to our lives.

My friend's twenty-four-year-old daughter Ellie became one of the estimated 12.6 million people who took in pets between March and December 2020, according to the American Pet Products Association. Ellie had been let go from her job and moved back home to her parents' apartment where she spent months watching all the dogs that were out and about in the neighborhood. She knew she wanted one of her own, but with demand so high, it took a long time before she was able to arrange for the adoption of Dolly. "She is the most amazing dog and she's changed my life," Ellie told me.

Like many new dog owners, Ellie felt great gratitude for the companionship of a pet during the pandemic. With lockdown and working from home, people began to dote on their pets. Social media feeds were filled with photos of dogs and cats, suddenly the most important members of the household. My sister-in-law Marcea forwarded me a meme of the family dog lying on the floor exhausted from too many walks and too much attention.

Our pets helped us process our grief during COVID. A few months after my friend Wendy lost her father to cancer, she welcomed a loving chocolate brown Labradoodle into her life. Named for Wendy's father, Abe went through training and certification and now makes weekly visits to the cancer ward at the local hospital, providing love, support, and snuggles for patients.

During the pandemic, I relied on two of my dearest friends, Gail and Suzy, who I met decades ago in college. These friendships were cemented forever by our four years on the idyllic Bloomington campus, by red Indiana University sweatshirts, and with red plastic cups of beer in our hands. Every May, like clockwork, I get a call or text from Suzy on the anniversary of our college graduation—a reminder of our many years of beautiful friendship and a blatant reminder of how freaking old we are! Old or not, there is no substitute for a friend who knows you and loves you—wrinkles, warts, and all.

It was Gail who years ago relayed something her daughter said to her. "Mom," her daughter said, "sometimes I don't need you to fix anything. I am just calling to vent!" A tidbit of wisdom that I should write on a Post-it note and paste to my forehead came from Gail, one of my wisest and wittiest friends. It continues to be a relevant reminder of my relationship with my own daughter. Gail called a few weeks before the holidays in 2020 to say, "I don't know what we're doing or what we'll be eating or drinking, but we're going to be celebrating, and we're going to be festive if it kills us!"

During this time, I was so thankful for the friendships in my life that allowed me to just be who I needed to be, no maintenance required, with out-of-the-box behavior always accepted.

"Mom, it's who you choose to surround yourself with that matters most," Andrew told me one Sunday evening after he came back from watching football with the guys. Grateful for the time together with his old buddies, he talked about how he and many of his friends had developed a deep appreciation for the ability to be together in person. They no longer take it for granted.

According to a February 2020 AARP survey, all generations agree that the top two benefits of friendship are having someone to share activities and experience life with, and having someone to talk to. Opinions across the generations, however, are more nuanced. Boomers are more likely to say they value sharing activities and life experiences with others. Gen X-ers, on the other hand, are more likely to rely on friends to help them solve problems. And Millennials are more likely to view friendships as part of a healthy lifestyle and a way to feel valued.

Millennials and Gen Z-ers who have grown up in a technological world have had the ability to stay connected to a large network of people, but through their collaborative and curious behavior, they are also deeply connected to their in-person relationships. Through my children, I have seen that the younger generations have deep and wonderful friendships with people of all ages who have been part of their lives and helped them grow—friends on whom they can rely for the good times as well as the tough times. We have all needed to navigate the changes in our lives, and many of us have learned how to find relational togetherness while being physically apart.

When it felt like we were standing still, many people gained new perspective and were grateful for the friendships that were strong enough to withstand the distance and separation, as well as the forced togetherness the pandemic created in our world. During a time of tragic disconnect, we identified the relationships that truly matter the most.

9

Faith Reimagined

Choose Faith over Fear

October 2020

Adrian

Handsome and healthy Tom Hanks, and his wife, Rita Wilson, were the first disclosed celebrities to contract COVID-19 and speak openly about their time in isolation in Australia. For many, this solidified that COVID was a reality. They spoke candidly about how their faith helped them champion the unknown outcome of the virus. Thankfully, they came out on the healthy side, but others were not as fortunate.

"Jenny's almost 101 years of life, born in 1920, was wrapped between two worldwide pandemics. Today, we remember her life," said the rabbi who was leading a virtual celebration of the life of the mother of my dear friend Daniela, my dancing buddy and caring community partner. I sat in the dentist chair with my ear pods in my ears, listening to Jenny's family share stories of her professional life working for the United Nations, her love affair with her husband, and the family's countless memories of her. Also known as Nana J, Jenny was born at the tail end of the Spanish flu epidemic and after World War I. It was a time of optimism and great uncertainty, and she left the world hoping for the end of the coronavirus pandemic during another era of great uncertainty.

When I received the group text that Nadine, one of my dearest friends, had just lost her father to a battle with stomach cancer, my heart was broken for her and her family. I felt a void as well—the loss of not being able to physically be there for Nadine. We had shared many conversations and texts while her father went through cancer treatment. My texts always concluded with sending my love and prayers. Just the immediate family attended the small funeral in New York.

The process of loss usually commences with a gathering of the mourners surrounded by "their people" to share memories, give hugs, and provide connection. Community warmth and the power of prayer are sources of comfort during challenging times. It's another example of people needing people. But during the pandemic, at a time when connection was so deeply needed, families, communities, and worship spaces were physically disconnected.

I am a spiritual woman, often referring to myself as a cultural Jew. I love my faith because it connects me to those who came before me. Some of my happiest memories revolve around traditions and holidays with my loved ones. I believe there is something bigger than all of us and that things happen for a reason. I also believe that in some instances, there is no explanation for why things happen. On those occasions, the Greater Power shares our pain.

Early in the pandemic, my friend Lisa, a cantor and clergy member, reminded me that faith must be constantly reimagined. At every critical juncture in history, faith has been tested. During the pandemic, her house of worship and clergy team had to reimagine how to keep the faith while the community could no longer gather in person. She and her colleagues had to "learn how to convey spirituality through a screen and how to be prayerful virtually."

A need for prayer was heightened among all demographics, and the ability to connect with a community of worship was very important to Lisa's congregants during this lonely time.

"God is crying for all of us," she told me. Despite all the suffering and sadness in our world, we must adapt, rethink, and have faith.

One rainy Saturday afternoon Kenny, Brian, and I sat on the sofa in our rental apartment, prepared with both tissues and snacks as we watched amazing Rabbi Judy share precious sentiments about our dear friends Leah and Matt, the couple standing before her under the chuppah. I have known Leah since she was three months old with her stick-straight hair, serious expression, a mind full of cautious curiosity, and the wit of a mature soul. The rabbi chanted the traditional Hebrew blessings and gave eloquent explanations about the spirituality and faith that comes into action when we find our significant other or soul mate. It is crazy how in this huge, diverse world, we somehow manage to meet and make what will hopefully be a lifelong commitment to another human being.

When I was a young woman, I always assumed I would get married someday. I had boyfriends but never had any thoughts about which boyfriend would be my lifelong partner. My relationship with Kenny just happened. We were set up by our mothers in 1984, and our long-distance love affair evolved into my relocation to Miami after I graduated from college. I moved to Miami without a thought about whether or not I had a ring on my finger. My top priority was to find a job, housing, a car, and all the items I needed to set up a life in a new city. Kenny had moved to Miami from Connecticut to attend the University of Miami and had already established roots while working for a local CPA firm. Having him there made my transition to Miami easier and more exciting.

One Monday night in February 1986 after a long workday, Kenny asked me to sit down on the bed and look under my pillow. I laughed and asked, "Did you lose a tooth or something?" Under the pillow I found a black velvet box, and when I looked back at Kenny, he was down on one knee in front of me.

"Will you marry me?" he asked with a serious yet sweet smile on his face.

I was totally surprised and shocked. Of course, I said yes.

Nine months later we were under the chuppah with my childhood rabbi from Kansas City, surrounded by our family and friends for a truly joyous occasion. I have often said that something bigger than us brought us together, or maybe I was so young and foolish that I didn't realize what was happening. Overall, the ease of our relationship from the very beginning has been unique. Even on the most frustrating days during the pandemic, it was clear that we were meant to share this life together. Whether I took a leap for love or a leap of faith, I am so grateful that we found each other.

For centuries, individuals have committed themselves to be half of the whole in a relationship. They meet organically or are introduced by common friends or through the swipe of a finger on a dating app. Relationships are created, and lives move forward. When the time is right and the link of love is solid, engagements commence, and plans for the dream wedding begin. The wedding fantasy often includes a few hundred people, a beautiful dress, flowers, and music in a church, in a synagogue, or at the beach. But in the age of COVID-19, weddings became huge headaches.

My friend Michelle, a wedding planner, shared that thousands of couples with weddings scheduled from mid-March 2020 and after had to either postpone their existing plans or downsize to a very intimate event. Some kept their plans alive, not believing that the pandemic would last very long. Then Michelle said, "When the date was only a few months or even weeks away, they quickly reimagined their wedding to comply with the COVID-19 guidelines."

Couples tried to find a wedding format that worked for them. Right or wrong, they were not going to reimagine their lives with their soon-to-be spouse or partner. When personal beliefs spoke louder than the suggested guidelines, couples went ahead and welcomed their guests into the wedding space and carried on as usual. That often resulted in what came to be known as "super-spreader" occasions.

For the most part, Michelle said, "Creativity and faith kicked in. Mini and micro weddings replaced traditional wedding plans, and the sanctity of marriage moved forward with pared-down guest lists, often with friends and family in the Zoom room. It actually felt as if the importance of the union of the couple was magnified with faith and love."

Our daughter Rachel was scheduled to attend the Valentine's Day wedding of Lexi, her best friend from summers at sleepaway camp. Originally planned in Philadelphia for over 200 guests, the wedding was scaled down to twenty family members and two friends. The couple grieved the loss of their original vision for their wedding festivities, but nothing was going to cause them to put off their nuptials. They were ready to get on with their life together, and they had their priorities in order. Their faith in one another, their family, and the universe that brought them together was greater than the pandemic. Faith prevailed even without the usual gathering of extended family and community.

"The ceremony took place outside, umbrellas open as sleet came down," Rachel recalled. "The very happy and chilly couple were surrounded by their loved ones in snow boots, furs, and masks. I felt honored to be asked to sign the Ketubah, the official Jewish marriage document that can't be signed by a family member."

"Man plans, and God laughs," the saying goes. So many plans were altered during the pandemic, yet the magnificence of these moments was exactly as it was meant to be.

I have always had friends of many faiths, and I have great admiration for the spiritual leaders of all religious traditions who worked during the pandemic to help reimagine communities, prayer, and rituals. In the early months of the pandemic, while drinking my morning coffee and reading *The New York Times*, my heart started beating anxiously as I read an article by James Estrin called "Staying Apart, But Praying Together." The article acknowledged many different faiths and how they provided spiritual guidance during this unprecedented time.

My heart ached when I read that nineteen members of the Christian Cultural Center, a mega church in East Brooklyn, New York, had died from COVID. Hundreds more were infected, including the pastor, Dr. A. R. Bernard, who said he spent a week in the hospital in March "with every symptom imaginable." Like many other large churches in New York City, the Christian Cultural Center closed its building in March 2020 because of deep concerns for the safety of its congregants. The church met the needs of the community even though they closed their doors. A daily prayer conference call attracted about 1,300 people every morning. "We are still doing community," Dr. Bernard said. "Isolation is antithetical to our sense of purpose. The building is closed, but church is open."

Daily and weekly worship services of all religions continued to take place online and in person, following the CDC guidelines. Study sessions and educational classes for all ages continued. My friend Mary's daughter, Anika, hosted a weekly Bible study group for young adults on her parents' boat in California. "Having the ocean and the great outdoors as the backdrop added a higher level of spirituality to the experience," Anika shared. Mary, who had been my college roommate, has always believed in faith over fear. That's how she managed to continue running an essential business during this very challenging time. Prayer sessions for the sick and suffering increased, with prayer vigils taking place in hospital parking lots for those sick with COVID-19 and for the medical professionals caring for the sick.

My cardiologist's nurse, Lissette, was sent home from work early in the pandemic with her personal items and her computer. "This was the beginning of the original 'lockdown,'" she said, making air quotes with her fingers. I had always loved visiting with Lissette a few times a year as she took my blood and hooked me up to the EKG machine. We discussed our families, and the conversation always landed on the topic of our faith. A member of the Seventh Day Adventist Church, Lissette drew on her faith throughout her pandemic journey. She faced confusion, fear, and financial concerns as she moved through her new COVID-19 reality. She worried about her elderly mother who had a heart condition and lived in the Dominican Republic. "If my mother gets sick, I can't get to her," Lissette said. Nevertheless, she recognized that everything became clearer during this time—the hardships and the goodness alike. "Even with masks on our faces, our souls can serve as our vision," she said.

Laura and I have had the opportunity to work with different faith-based organizations in our Good Work Miami roles. Faith is deep, different, and sometimes difficult. The core beliefs and values quite often have remained the same throughout the generations, but the congregants have evolved over the decades. We have witnessed that the passion for faith has remained the same, but our value of time has changed. The older we get, the more time becomes a coveted currency. The younger generation wants to go to mass or Shabbat service, feel connected to the traditions, hear words of inspiration from the clergy, say hello to a few fellow congregants, and be on their way in approximately forty-two minutes. The same time crunch is present in the board room of these faith-based congregations. When leading a board retreat in early 2020 for a group of young, high-level professionals, they shared with Laura and me that they did not want to go "into the weeds" with any conversation. They wanted to process the issue at hand, make a decision, and move on. Their philosophy was to be efficient, effective, and on task. They were so smart and yet so different from our generation of board members. Wanting everyone's voice to be included, we would go into the weeds, pick the flowers, and mow the lawn all at the same time.

In retrospect, that particular board retreat for a large organization was our aha moment into what our adult children were teaching us in our own homes during this time. Worship services, life cycle events, and study groups on Zoom or outdoors for all faiths were fulfilling and efficient, aligned with the younger generation's philosophy. Maybe it was an ongoing option for the future. The pandemic touched all of us, whatever our denomination. We may have suffered differently and found joy differently, but faith played an important role, no matter how it was reimagined.

10

On the Dock

The Best Things in Life Are Simple

November 2020

Laura

Pre-pandemic, I ran through life, moving a mile a minute. I didn't run necessarily for my health and well-being, although I always plugged exercise into my day. I was busy sprinting from place to place, from person to person, wanting to please everyone and miss nothing. When the world stopped, the days were long and felt like a marathon of unknowns. Living in South Florida surrounded by water was a gift that somehow I had taken for granted. Although the open-water dock down the street from our house had always been there, I didn't quite appreciate it the way I did in the winter of 2020. This period of time taught me to slow down, be in the moment, and treasure the time with my adult children.

Like many in 2020, my son Andrew spent a ton of time exercising. Not new to the whole endurance sports culture, I have spent a good chunk of my marriage hearing the alarm sound at ungodly hours. When Dan and I met back in the

'80s, he and his brother were doing triathlons and training for his first New York City marathon.

Thirty years later, in 2016, Dan registered to run it again, this time with our two sons Jacob and Andrew. We flew to New York for a fall family weekend, and as Emily and I stood on First Avenue on a glorious blue-sky day watching the spectacle of marathoners making their way past the sixteen-mile marker, it became apparent that we were witnessing a natural passing of the baton. Dan, a four-time marathon finisher, was getting tired, and the twenty-somethings still had fresh legs.

With less fanfare than one would expect from an endurance athlete starting to slow down—realizing in real time that maybe he should just accept that he'd "had a good run"—Dan turned his attention to our younger son Andrew. Ten miles later, both our sons crossed the Central Park finish line, looking remarkably good and even seeming to have a little gas left in the tank.

Legend has it that there was an epic brotherly conversation at the 21-mile marker at about Fifth Avenue and 138th Street where Jacob apparently hit the wall, sat down on the curb, and said, "I'm done." With what I affectionately call the "Andrew Koffsky motivational speech of a lifetime," the younger brother somehow managed to convince the older brother to "get up; we are not coming back here to do this race again." Both brothers laugh when they tell the story, reflecting on those pivotal moments when it could have gone either way. Jacob says that given Andrew's relentlessness and his sheer persistence in getting in his brother's face, there was no way he could give up.

One of the greatest gifts in my life is to be a mother of sons. Loud, sweaty, stinky, and often with things breaking and crashing, boys in the house are never dull and are truly a gift. Having grown up in a girl household, I was completely mesmerized watching Jacob as a little boy. Almost immediately, he gravitated to all things transportation. "Mommy, cement mixer!" he blared from his car seat, holding a Hot Wheel in each of his little hands. At home, he carried around his most prized possession—a black plastic box with trays and compartments that held his beloved cars. He knew the make and model of each car. For hours he sat and played, vrooming his cars back and forth.

I remember Jacob's elation one birthday when my mother gave him a Fisher Price parking garage that came with a variety of colored cars, ramps, and even an elevator. During his Brio train phase, he set up elaborate train tracks with twists and bridges while little Andrew sat shotgun next to him and watched everything his big brother did. Two years apart, they were each other's very first playmate, a built-in buddy to have throughout their lives. Whether it was who got the ball first or who got the bigger piece of pizza, everything was always a competition.

For many years, I peered out the window to see the two of them guarding each other, practicing layups in our driveway. Every afternoon featured the steady Zen-like beat of the basketball until inevitably it was interrupted, usually by one of them complaining that someone had cheated or miscalculated the score. There would be cursing, criticism, and often a punch. "You suck!" Andrew said before slamming the door. "You suck!" Jacob retorted. But within minutes, they were sitting together on the couch playing a game or watching a TV show together and laughing. Through middle school, high school, summer camp, and college, they were each other's best friend. They were very different individuals but also similar in so many ways. They were always there for one another.

While Jacob's marathon days were "one and done," Andrew, after months of living cooped up in COVID lockdown, became interested in getting into endurance sports. He decided he was going to train for the Orlando Half Ironman. The training required discipline, along with physical and mental strength, and it gave Andrew something to focus on during the pandemic. This was his way of trying to have control in an uncontrollable time.

Andrew scheduled his training, allocating time to run, bike, and swim. Each week he increased his miles incrementally. He bought a wet suit and did early morning swims in Biscayne Bay. During those many months when we waited for the vaccines to roll out and welcomed anything that presented itself as a diversion from the harshness of our country's political divide, Andrew's half Ironman became something that sustained us all. We took collective pride in his training regimen and looked forward to his morning mileage check-in, a text, or a photo updating us on what he had accomplished, usually before the rest of us had even had our first cup of coffee.

Thrilled that my hubby had a buddy to wake up and run or bike with, I often heard them early in the morning in the kitchen, laughing and discussing all the logistics like it was a 6:00 a.m. happy hour. Dinner conversations became a family affair as we listened to Andrew discuss his plans for the next day's exercise and review details for meals, snacks, and hydration.

Like much of 2020, things didn't always go according to plan, and the Half Ironman race was canceled. So Andrew decided he was going to run his own Half Ironman race on Thanksgiving morning and raise money for Experience Camps. It was a nonprofit network of no-cost camps that help grieving children thrive by building their coping resources, confidence, and resilience. Andrew and his siblings had volunteered for it many summers.

As moms, most of us have moments with our children that stand out in our minds—some good, some not so good. But on that Thanksgiving morning in 2020, I saw the result of all those years of trying to instill positive values in our kids, as well as those sibling bonds we had worked so hard to create. We all knew how important this was for Andrew, and the team rallied. They were all in.

If the COVID time taught me anything, I learned that we must be adaptable. I had to get onboard, too, and put on my giant, Party City, rose-colored, cheerleading glasses. I had to realize it was time to be a passenger on the Team Andrew bus. Emily instantly got onboard, literally paddle-boarding next to her brother in the bay, shooting videos, posting live updates on Instagram, and dropping the fundraising link into every creative caption.

Michael, one of Andrew's friends, drove an hour that morning just to ride his bike with Andrew, pacing him for the entire 56-mile bike segment. Dan, Jacob, and Steph, none of whom were in racing shape, divvied up the miles and relayed around the course, making sure Andrew had someone running alongside him during the 13.1 miles. Friends followed him throughout the bike route, drove next to him, cheered him on, and gave him encouragement. The entire thing had a very Ferris Bueller-esque feel to it, and when it was over, the team had raised more than $14,000.

One night a few weeks later, I thought I recognized the "Age of Aquarius" playing on a portable speaker as Emily came down the stairs. "Mom," she asked, "have you heard of the group the Fifth Dimension?"

"Have I heard of the Fifth Dimension?" I shot right back. Was she kidding me? "I actually saw the Fifth Dimension live in concert!" I said with my hands on my hips. Standing in the kitchen, I told her the story of how my mother and father took my sisters and me to see the Fifth Dimension live in 1970 at the Jackie Gleason Theater in Miami Beach. The group was decked out in their powder-blue polyester costumes. She beamed, and it occurred to me that it really is true that "everything old is new again."

I put some paper cups, a bag of Doritos, and a bottle of rosé wine into a bag. Emily was taking a break from studying for finals, and we headed to the dock at the end of the street where we had the best view of the moon on that December night. Throughout the many months of the pandemic, the dock was our little secluded slice of heaven, our sanctuary overlooking the bay, giving us an opportunity to sit and slow down and just breathe in the open air.

In the mornings as we watched the sun rise, Dan, the kids, and I would sip our morning cup of coffee before delving into the daily Zooms. But often we ended the day right back at the same place on the dock, cocktails in hand at sunset. We made elaborate charcuterie and cheese boards, each person using their own plastic utensils and having their own individual Ziploc baggies of crackers in order not to spread any potential COVID germs.

I also hosted my girlfriends on the dock. We took off our masks and caught up on each other's lives. We brought out our folding table and wheeled out a cooler full of beer, wine, and whatever we cooked or ordered for dinner. Instantly, the dock with the backdrop of the bay was the perfect vibe for a Saturday night get-together with friends. We celebrated birthdays there, lit candles on cakes, marked the milestones, enjoyed the view, and took in the vastness of the open water. The dock had always been there, but somehow during the many days of the pandemic, our perspectives changed.

One night there was a conjunction of Jupiter and Saturn. Those two planets had not appeared that close together from Earth's vantage point since 1623, back when Galileo was still alive. An astronomical conjunction occurs when any two heavenly bodies appear to pass or meet each other as seen from Earth.

"Mom, do you understand the significance of this?" Emily asked as we gazed at the heavens. "It's about manifesting our vision for what we want our world to be."

With cups in hand under the most magnificent moonlit sky and the sounds of "Let the Sunshine In" playing into the night, the two of us had our little Great Conjunction gratitude dance party on the dock. What a gift it was to have this time together. It had been years since Dan and I had lived with the steady pulse of a full house. Here we were with our kids again, only this time it wasn't frenetic. We were in the moment, taking it all in, grateful and aware that there is nothing better than spending time with our children.

As 2020 drew to a close, we celebrated Jacob's birthday as we do every New Year's Eve. For me, it's always a day of reflection on the passage of time. This birthday marked my oldest son's last year of his 20s. We sat side by side, sipping champagne in our red cups, our legs dangling over the dock. Fully in the moment, I felt so fortunate to have a few moments to check in with him (although I was also thinking about Louie and whether he was a dog that would freak out at the sound of the upcoming fireworks). Jacob was now a new husband and a new lawyer. I could see the dark circles under his eyes.

"Learning to find the balance in life is challenging," I said.

Sitting on the dock in that moment, I felt like I was literally watching my son grow into a man right before my eyes. We talked about our new hybrid, flexible working world. I listened to him lay out his professional goals and the challenges he and his friends were confronting, and I saw the adult version of the little boy Dan and I had raised. He was smart, humble, pragmatic, open-minded, optimistic, and funny. As I heard his words, I realized how much my role as a parent was changing. While I had real-life experiences and opinions, I didn't have any answers for the issues he was now confronting. These were his issues and his choices to make, and I was confident that my son could and would figure out what was right for himself. My role was shifting to "best supporting actress," and he was now the lead role in charge of his own life. He was as prepared as he could be for the world that awaited him.

COVID had given us an unexpected gift—unstructured time in which deep, substantive conversations could arise—and we were grateful our kids still wanted to spend time with us. We must have done something right. Sitting on the dock, I wonder what experiences my kids will remember throughout their lives. I hope we have been able to instill in them the most important lessons for life and that we have imparted a sense of responsibility to give back.

Young parents work so hard, going a mile a minute with so much to prove and never wanting to miss a thing. As we get older, we learn to slow down, and we know how quickly it all goes. COVID-19 gave us an unobstructed vantage point. It magnified how fragile life is and gave us the perspective to know that we cannot take anything for granted. The trivial things that once consumed us are insignificant in the scheme of what we now know is important. Will we remain conscious of this gift once the crisis has passed, or we will boomerang right back to our over-programmed lives, moving from one thing to the next without intention?

11

The Great Outdoors

Breathe Deeply, and Be Present

January 2021

Adrian

I was full of optimism and intention on January 20, 2021, while much of the country spent a good portion of the day glued to the television as Joe Biden, the forty-sixth president of the United States, and Kamala Harris, the forty-ninth vice president, were sworn into office on a day that felt ripe with the promise of hope. The inauguration was repurposed to be outdoors and in alignment with social distance standards, but the heartfelt passion for our country and for those who serve it with honor, intention, and optimism was apparent.

During the inauguration, there were snippets of loving sentiments for poet laureate Amanda Gorman's beautiful words and fabulous yellow coat. At 8:30 in the evening, the Boss, Bruce Springsteen, sang "Land of Hope and Dreams" at the Lincoln Memorial. Does it get any better than that?

It did get better as we entered 2021 grateful to be survivors of the COVID-19 pandemic. "If you think you know where you will be one year from today, rethink it," was the final sentiment shared by Sydney, the SoulCycle instructor at our Saturday morning rooftop spin class. This resonated so deeply with me, as well as with Rachel, because it was nearly a year since our crazy coronavirus chaos had begun. On the drive across the causeway to spin class that morning, we reminisced about day one of this journey that had become so familiar during the past few months. The causeway was filled with the usual walkers, bikers, scooter riders, and skateboarders, which made me uber cautious behind the wheel. We admired the beautiful weather, the boats in the water, and the new styles of athleisure attire on the people we passed.

"Look how many women are wearing athleisure skorts," Rachel commented. "They're so comfortable for all types of exercise, not just tennis."

We arrived at our destination and then took the elevator to the parking garage rooftop where fifty spin bikes were set up at least six feet apart and sanitized before and after each class. Before signing in, we used the ladies' room, wondering why there was such a nice ladies' room on the roof of a parking garage. Before the pandemic, had we never peed in a bathroom on the roof of a parking garage. We checked in, got our shoes, towels, and headphones, and mounted our bikes after adjusting them to fit our frames.

"Mom, are you good?" Rachel asked, knowing that I was always a bit timid regarding my spinning skills. "You'll do great," she said in her positive cheerleader voice.

The sun was bright, and the breeze was nice, but the vibe of the class was special. We had survived almost a year living in a pandemic. We were healthy, and we were taking a spin class—not in the usual pre-COVID small dark studio but in the bright light and open air.

"Breathe deeply in and out; pace yourself" were Rachel's last words before the music blasted and our peddling pleasure began. The sweat brought stress relief and smiles.

Our pandemic journey through the coronavirus lunacy had been a bit more manageable because of our location in Florida where we could be in the great outdoors year round. Spending time outside deepened relationships, saved marriages, and helped our overall health and happiness, leaving us with a greater appreciation for nature and each other.

I have always loved being outdoors. Growing up in Kansas, I felt liberated when spring arrived and I could play outside without the constraint of a winter coat. Summer was the best. Scents of happy times from my early childhood summers are still present in my memory bank and occasionally reactivated today. Those memories include the smell of chlorine at the neighborhood pool; fresh-cut grass underfoot as we ran around in the backyard catching fireflies in Mason jars; and watermelon triangles with a sprinkle of salt, a popular summer dessert usually eaten before bedtime.

When fall arrived, I remember the crunch of leaves under our feet as my brother Brent and I played kick-the-can or freeze tag with the neighborhood kids on our cul-de-sac. We played outside until our faces were red from the chill in the air and our parents called us in for dinner with a whistle tune that was unique to our family. Winter was a bit more challenging, but sledding on the hill behind our house was always fun, followed by hot cocoa with marshmallows in front of the fireplace in the family room.

Fresh air felt good in my childhood, and during COVID, as the virus dominated every day and businesses came to a halt, it seemed as if everyone started taking walks outside because the fresh air felt so good. Morning, evening, throughout the day— we never saw so many people walking as we did in those early weeks of COVID. It's as if the whole world was desperate to be outdoors, move their bodies, and breathe fresh, clean air. I thought if I could breathe in fresh air and was at least twenty feet away from another person, I would stay healthy and strong, and the virus monster could not catch me. Crazy, crazy, and crazier!

Since so many families like mine had welcomed their adult children back home and everyone was working in their separate corners, we had walk-and-talks (business meetings or catchups), walk-and-pods (listening to a podcast), social distance walks with friends, fat-burning walks, high-intensity walks, and simple strolls—all just to escape. I definitely looked freaky with a bandana around my neck (doubling as a wrinkle guard), a mask over my face, a ponytail, hat, sunscreen on top of old sunscreen, glasses, fanny pack—all facilitating the look of ugly, ugly, and uglier.

But escaping to the great outdoors was absolutely necessary for my mental, physical, and emotional well-being. It feels a bit shallow now to share how focused we were on exercise for sustenance, especially as the virus continued to cause tragic health challenges for so many. The reality was that we needed to move our bodies more than ever. We needed the dopamine and endorphins—the chemicals that are released in our brains when we exercise and make us happy. We needed happy! Pre-pandemic, we had made our "happy time" a priority as often as possible, but during this bizarre time, we needed it more than ever. We became gluttons for exercise and sports, enjoying the high however we could get it.

By the third week of March 2020, the parks limited walking. Paths and par courses, gyms, spinning studios, dance studios, tennis courts, and golf courses all closed. Despite being individual sports, all these activities involved the use of common equipment and included human contact. It was traumatic when we heard the news that the golf courses were closed. Golf had been the outlet that gave my entire family a happy pause.

Kenny and Brian became a cluster of frustration in the house on weekend mornings without their usual golf expedition. They shifted their energies to tracking daily steps. How many steps they took every day became an obsession for all of us. The Quaranteam, fully donned in sweat-resistant attire and masks, headed to the streets, usually after our second cup of coffee. Walking as a family pack gave us a ridiculous amount of quality time together ruminating about "what's next" or all the things we thought we could control.

We had BooMillennial moments during our walks, discussing political divisiveness and the incidents that brought heightened awareness to racial injustice and diversity. We shared our concerns about climate change, noting that lockdown was beneficial for our environment. We shared deep thoughts about history from the Boomer perspective and listened intently to the comments of our wise Millennials. We reapplied our sunscreen, drank tons of water, found unique places to relieve our bladders, and admired the manatees in the ocean. At the end of the day, all of us had extremely fatigued feet.

The great outdoors had a different meaning for others due to the economic, physical, and mental effects of COVID-19. In neighborhoods throughout the country, including ours, the homeless population marked their parcels of grass with folding chairs and shopping carts filled with their possessions. One woman riddled with spinal disease took possession of a public bus stop as her home. We passed her daily on our walks, often waving in acknowledgment. She could not see our expressions under our masks, but her reality made us feel helpless and sad.

In South Florida, shelters became increasingly dangerous because of COVID, so people moved outside. Other parts of the country with harsher weather had greater issues and had to provide indoor housing alternatives. Before the pandemic, rates of homelessness were the highest they'd been in the United States in twenty years. COVID increased those numbers, leaving people without money, shelter, or food. People were hungry, and it was heartbreaking.

"I need to do something," Brian said one afternoon. Brian hosts an annual walk in New York City—Brian's Boogie Down Broadway—a 13.3-mile walk down Broadway that he initiated a few years ago for fundraising and friend-raising purposes. The funds raised went to a worthy cause, and Brian's event gave participants the unique experience of walking the Island of Manhattan from top to bottom. There were always stops along the way for refreshments.

The walk ended downtown at one of the local bars where everyone shared accomplishments and camaraderie. During the pandemic, Brian's Boogie Down Broadway became a virtual event with the help of the Strava App, an Internet service for tracking human exercise. Boogie participants all over the country tracked their independent walks, raising money to provide food for the homeless population and those with food insecurities.

During that time, new virtual exercise options entered the fitness world. Trainers and coaches held their classes and one-on-one sessions on Zoom. Taryn Toomey's "The Class," a famous New York City exercise routine, played on many screens of both Millennials and extremely fit Boomers. Brian encouraged me to join him and introduced me to this definitely-not-for-this-Boomer class on our rooftop patio at 7:00 a.m. He mirrored the instructor's moves with precision and strength while I barely finished the painful burpees followed by planking to death. I was soon done for the day.

Rachel and I took virtual dance classes on our rooftop, on our balcony, and in our living room. We found our favorite dance instructor on YouTube and followed along like spastic showgirls. Sometimes we made up our own steps and belted out the song lyrics in unison. When we finished, we completed the workout session with another YouTube called "Eight-Minute Abs" led by an Art Linkletter voice-double that was probably made thirty years ago. We also laughed our way through Jane Fonda's 1980s workout and her motivating expression, "You grew it. You lift it!" That was during the awful doggie-style leg lifts of my college era. We've come a long way from doing the Jane Fonda VHS on my shag carpet.

Virtual yoga and pilates sessions kept us stretching and strong. Peloton and SoulCycle bikes were delivered all over the country. Communities were created through the instructors and fellow spinners who were shaping fit bodies. As Laura once said with a warm smile, "It felt as if the participants were my dear friends, and I wanted to have the instructor over for dinner." There were several months when the wait for delivery of these two-wheeled bicycle contraptions was six months. The manufacturers could not produce them quickly enough.

Brian has often found happiness in unusual, goal-driven initiatives. I can still remember the feeling in my stomach several years before the pandemic when my son told me he had won the lottery for the New York City Marathon and was going to run 26.2 miles on November 4, 2018. I shared my concern first and then my excitement, not really believing that this would come to fruition. But it did, and we were there to support him with our love, cheers, signs, and craziness. After he crossed the finish line and went through the cool-down rituals, we couldn't wait to shower him with our hugs and pride. The following year, he ran the Chicago Marathon, followed by other races and events with multiple activities. Brian and I even ran the Disney Half-Marathon in January 2020. He chose to run at his mother's slower pace so we could share the experience together. So sweet, right?

On a Monday evening several weeks into the pandemic, Brian and Laura's son Andrew took a walk-and-talk together at the park, which caused Brian to get home a bit late for dinner. After he apologized and we became accustomed to his lovely, sweaty smell at the dinner table, he announced, "Drewbie and I just signed up to do an Ironman in July 2021."

"How are you guys changing the world this week?" I asked. This was the usual dialogue between Andrew, Brian, and about five other buddies who got together for scheduled Monday evening conversations. These conversations, I was told, were filled with depth, feeling, and thoughts about how to make positive change in the world, especially during the dark days of the pandemic. As Brian's mother, I loved that my son had the ability to connect at a deep level with other young men who were like-minded and interesting. I had no idea what signing up for an Ironman was. I truly thought it sounded ambitious, inspiring, and just a lovely plan of action. I was soon to discover that Brian and Andrew had a plan of action, yes, but lovely it was not.

An Ironman is an international athletic competition for lunatics who want to kill their mothers. It is a triathlon that entails a 2.4-mile swim, a 112-mile bicycle ride, and a 26.2-mile run, totaling 140.6 miles of physical and mental movement. I thought Brian was kidding, and in my usual mother mode, I professed my support with my cheerleader pom-pom-shaking attitude.

Within months, the Ironman chatter became more frequent and louder, detailing the equipment needed and the training process, including nutritional supplements and specific foods. Totally in denial that my amazing son who had come from my non-athletic loins would really embark on this ridiculous training journey, I was still very casually conversant about his goal.

Then the equipment began to arrive, including a super-snazzy bike and the silly-looking attire that goes with it. A few weeks later, a variety of swim gear was delivered, including kickboards and flippers. Brian's nutritional requirements made their way onto my grocery list. Organic everything, including coffee—and hydration, hydration, hydration followed by urination, urination, urination. He peed like a racehorse all day long; I could hear his toilet flush between his work calls. My workspace was right next to his bathroom.

Brian was a runner, so we will give him that in his athletic column. But on the first day that he went out on that snazzy bike and took off with Andrew for a long and meaningful bike ride, the telephone rang, and we heard the news that Brian had fallen. He was able to call us, so we knew he was alive, but I lost ten years of my life waiting to see my baby boy. Thank goodness Kenny was home to retrieve our ambitious son who was able to walk into the house although he was pretty banged up with scrapes and bruises where the sun doesn't shine.

After a shower, ice, Advil, and a complete body check by his father, Brian parked himself on the sofa for the weekend. Of course, I loved that because I was by his side catering to his every need while watching movies together. In the back of my mind, I was hopeful that this Ironman nonsense was over. Boy, was I wrong. Brian was more determined than ever and now recognized that he needed help to train for this lofty feat. He did his research and found a team of triathletes. A few weeks later, training began. At this point I realized how motivated and fully focused Brian was on achieving his goal.

Brian and Andrew, together and apart in the great outdoors that only South Florida offers in the heart of winter, began the physical, mental, emotional, and nutritional training to accomplish their goal. Their lifetime friendship was one of trust and respect. They were comfortable with each other's character, knowing their core values were aligned even though their athletic skills were not. Andrew comes from a family of intense athletes; Brian comes from our family—relaxed athletes. Our mantra has always been "if you had fun, you won." That does not make for an Ironman.

When Brian and Andrew were old enough to play in the popular basketball league at our synagogue, they were on opposing teams for the first game of the season. The adorable eight-year-olds arrived at the basketball court, their coaches assigned them uniforms, and into the bathroom they went to change. It was a very exciting moment for these new superstars. As the teams did their pre-game warmup drills, Andrew looked across the court and saw Brian in a pair of shorts that were too small for his thicker body. Then Andrew realized that his assigned shorts were too big on his skinny frame. Andrew grabbed Brian and led him into the bathroom where the swapping of the shorts took place. Of course, I followed them into the bathroom since I needed to see what this mad bathroom dash was all about.

When I arrived, I saw two little pishers in their cartoon tushy underpants, switching shorts so each boy had a more comfortable alternative. Even at a young age, they knew each other well and had an innate sense of deep friendship and camaraderie. The same was true during their many months of Ironman prep. Brian fell off his bike and fixed his issues by acquiring a coach. Andrew was thoughtful and meticulous in designing his training plan. He researched for hours, watched YouTubes, listened to podcasts, and followed the practices of other extreme athletes. The boys trained independently and differently, connecting almost daily to provide one another with coaching, confidence, and comfort.

Meanwhile, Laura and I spent many hours wondering why they needed to do this. Why couldn't they just solve world hunger in a way that kept them out of the ocean, off of their bikes, and safe and sound? We realized that they were a dynamic duo and that this ridiculous goal gave them a healthy focus that felt good during a time of so many unknowns. While I was a far cry from those carefree years, preferring to catch the glow of fireflies on warm summer nights with family, I was so grateful for the gift of family, friendship, and the great outdoors.

12

Aging Gratefully

Grow Old with Gratitude and Grace

March 2021

Laura

O n the one-year anniversary of the coronavirus being officially declared a global pandemic, Andrew drove his eighty-three-year-old grandmother to get a COVID-19 test. It was a couple days before she would head back to Connecticut. She had been in Florida for a nice long visit, braving the flight down with her dog in tow. When she arrived, she received hugs from her children and grandchildren in sunny Miami, a welcome change of scenery for her. During the year, she had finally received both vaccinations, and now she was ready to return home.

Andrew and his grandmother pulled up to the testing site. There were no lines and no waiting—a big change from the previous months when the lines snaked around the block as people waited for healthcare workers to approach their cars. The workers wore face shields and hazmat suits like something out of a sci-fi movie. Now grandmother and grandson stood in an open parking lot where those workers were swabbing noses and mouths, placing their sealed test tubes carefully in plastic pouches, and putting them in designated drop-off bins. It had all become normalized. With rapid Millennial-precision keystrokes, Andrew helped his grandmother fill in the fields of information and scan the confirmation barcode on her phone. The test results would be emailed to her in less than twenty-four hours.

Three of my friends lost their fathers during 2020. One died from complications from COVID-19. The other two were men in their late eighties, and although their passings were expected, their losses were painful. The inability to have a "normal" funeral—an observance to gather together to process the loss—made it almost impossible to find closure. Even before the pandemic, I never took anything for granted, but the year 2020 had indelibly cemented my perspective and given me greater appreciation for every simple and miraculous thing in life.

On my father's eighty-fifth birthday, we were all vaccinated and could gather in person to celebrate. He was healthy and as energetic as ever. We had made it through. My sister and brother-in-law got on a plane from Dallas to come and surprise him, and when he saw them, his eyes welled with tears. At a big table for ten at his favorite Miami restaurant, he was surrounded by his whole family. There were toasts, poems, an ice cream cake, and a video montage my niece put together with photos, songs, and recorded sentiments from all the kids and grandkids. We played it for him on an iPad.

The restaurant was loud, so we waited until we left our table and ushered him to a quieter area so he would be able to hear. There, sitting on a bench with all of us gathered around him, he listened to the words and watched the images of a life blessed with family. Births, proms, weddings, family vacations, Thanksgivings, days spent sitting on the couch or lingering at the table, and just being together—they were special moments and ordinary moments that, when we look back, make up a life. Frank Sinatra's inimitable "Fly Me to the Moon" played as the video ended. Sitting on the bench, my father was overwhelmed with emotion. Each of us was aware of the simplicity and the magnitude of the moment. What greater gift than to be able to share the words in our hearts and look back on the legacy we leave to those we love.

"I have learned that I can be happy with a much smaller life," my mother said to me one day while we sat outside on a breezy Mother's Day morning eating bagels. "Staying healthy, staying in touch with loved ones, and looking forward to better days ahead has been my mantra," she said. "I want to remain strong and independent. I want to be able to travel. I want to be able to adapt to the 'new normal,' and there *will* be a new normal," she shared with the certainty that can only come from having lived more than eighty years of life. For most of my life, I have been fortunate to have my parents living nearby, and during COVID, it was a gift for me and my daughter Emily to have my mother, her Grandma Dortie, living close to us.

When Emily was in high school, she and I loved watching the TV show *House of DVF*. The series followed the glamorous life of fashion icon Diane von Furstenberg. It's been my joke that style skips a generation. While my wardrobe is basically black, white, and navy with a smattering of yellow, my mother and daughter both have a much bolder, brighter fashion sense. One day, Grandma called to say she had a few things in her closet she'd like to give to Emily. We put on our masks and popped right over to her apartment. There we were, three generations in a global pandemic, having a try-on party in Dortie's closet.

"Emily, I bought this in New York in 1990. It's a Bob Mackie. Do you know who that is?" my mother asked.

"He was the famous designer who created clothes for Cher," I chimed in.

"Yes, he did," my mother said, "and some of his designs were really outrageous and some more subdued. But Emily, throughout my life I have found that more important than what you wear is to wear it with self-confidence." What wisdom from an extraordinary woman. At eighty-three years old, my mother still looked fabulous.

Emily slipped into her grandmother's dress, and it fit her perfectly.

"You look stunning, Em," my mother said as she pulled Emily's hair back behind her ears in an up-do fashion. "You're ready to go to a gala."

Even with reading glasses and a face mask on, I couldn't conceal my tears. Although none of us was going to a gala anytime soon, the moment was magical.

Over the years, my mother has often shared many principles that shaped her life. An only child, she has always spoken with gratitude about her mother, my Grandma Sue. With a kind heart and a fantastic sense of humor, my parents often said that Grandma Sue had the intellect to achieve greatness had she been born in another generation. My sisters and I remember our Grandma Sue as the woman who, when she babysat, never told on us if we left dishes in the sink or if we were late for curfew. At maybe 5 feet tall, she was feisty as hell, standing on the bleachers in the old Orange Bowl stadium screaming "Defense!" for her beloved Miami Dolphins. She was an original, and so is my mother.

My mother and father have always been respectfully involved in the lives of my sisters and me, including our spouses and children. But during the pandemic, they hesitantly began taking most of their "marching order" guidelines from us, including where it was safe to go and how many people they could be with at a time. This was a big shift for all of us, and with our adult children home, they were privy to all the nuances. The synergy across the generations was remarkable.

"Millennials are idealistic; Boomers are more pragmatic," my mother told me. "Aging gives us insight and wisdom for our priorities," she went on. "As a member of the older generation, I feel like I should absolutely *not* get out of the way. I still have a lot to learn and a lot to impart to the younger generations. The important thing for seniors is to stay relevant, read, have hobbies, and listen to all that is going on around us."

My mother has set an amazing example of how to gracefully step back while still being present and relevant. When she was in her forties and fifties, she was always polished and completely comfortable at the podium, a pioneer leader in the arts and Jewish philanthropic communities. Excellent at setting her vision and delegating to empower others to flex and grow, she was equally confident in knowing when to make space for her successor to step forward. As a mom, she also had that same sense of tempo—available but not intrusive—and except when one of us was traveling, hardly a day went by without us talking to each other.

Though her life funneled down to "smaller" during the pandemic, my mother's life will never be small. As she dashed into the gourmet grocery store in her perfectly coiffed hair and attire with her clutch handbag tucked neatly under her arm, it was apparent to me that the pandemic only gave my mother more perspective, appreciation, and independence. It also gave her the technical skills to continue playing bridge and attend meetings, classes, exhibits, and concerts online. She fully embraced the limitations that COVID-19 presented, just as she intentionally embraced the "new normal" of our future.

13

The Power of the Pause

Time Is Our Greatest Treasure

March 2021

Adrian

"One more episode?" Kenny asked.

"Yes!" I told my husband with excitement, even though it was almost midnight, an hour past our usual bedtime. We had already binged on three episodes that evening while eating our favorite ice cream. Kenny loves chocolate, and I like vanilla with chocolate stuff in it—the more stuff, the better.

"Do we have any popcorn?" he asked.

"Really? You're still hungry?" I asked. Did we need more nourishment for this marathon binge-watching session to get us to the finish line?

No, we were just happy to sit on our sofa with snacks in hand and enjoy watching hours and hours of streaming television together. We've always had TV shows we enjoyed and common interests, but the pandemic pause connected us with series, movies, documentaries, entertainment, and each other in a way that was unique to our relationship. And sharing the same space every day with only a wall between us came with a few frustrations, but overall, we became deeply acquainted with each other's multifaceted selves. With the remote control in hand while rewinding, fast forwarding, pausing, and playing, we found peace and pleasure as we enjoyed our time together on the sofa during the pandemic pause.

While having dinner at one of my favorite outdoor restaurants with my very wise friend Karen, I shared that I felt like I have had two opportunities to pause during my lifetime—the year I went through cancer treatment and the pandemic.

"Your life has never been on pause," she replied. "You were busy fighting for your life the first time, and the pandemic has made you more focused on priorities than ever before."

I had never thought of it that way. My definition of *pause* was jumping off the usual merry-go-round of life and spending more time withdrawn at home. Neither pause was planned—they just happened and sent me into full survivor mode.

During my cancer pause, I worked very hard to save my life with surgeries and chemotherapy treatments. I was fully active battling the disease, which I accomplished while acquiring a great deal of perspective, self-awareness, and gratitude.

During the pandemic pause, the world was collectively battling a tragic virus.

It caused a heightened awareness of both crushing sadness and the unbelievable goodness in our world. It gave us a hunger for knowledge, as well as unscripted growth, compassionate humanity, appreciation for our loved ones, and transformation like never before. Everyone has experienced some level of trauma from the collateral effects of COVID-19, but it also prompted post-traumatic growth, which suggests that people can emerge from trauma even stronger. The crisis ignited our innate resilience and honed our ability to bounce back quickly from challenges.

In an article by Kirsten Weir, "Life after COVID-19: Making Space for Growth," published by the American Psychological Association in 2020, I learned that post-traumatic growth theory was developed in the 1990s by psychologists Richard Tedeschi and Lawrence Calhoun. The theory of post-traumatic growth suggests that people can "emerge from trauma or adversity having achieved positive personal growth."

This view was also shared by my friend Joanne, a licensed clinical therapist who observed that in the wake of the pandemic, resilience and post-traumatic growth were taking place across all demographics. "An individual's ability to be resilient during traumatic times in life is an acquired ability," Joanne said, honed through experiencing multiple traumas and reframing thoughts.

My mom, JoAnn, is a true example of the potential for post-traumatic growth. In December 2019 she moved from Las Vegas to Fort Lauderdale to live closer to me in an independent living community. Mom has survived great losses and challenges during her lifetime, which has given her the ability to cope with unfortunate circumstances with admirable resilience. Within days at her new home, she made many friends and participated in a variety of activities. She was happy and excited to begin this new chapter of her life. This came to a sudden stop in March 2020 when lockdown began. Nevertheless, she was very good about keeping herself busy in her apartment. We had our weekly visits when I delivered groceries. She came out of the building with her shopping cart, fully dolled up with makeup and mask, and blowing air kisses and giving air hugs.

Mom had a vision for a connectivity and friendship club called Schmoozing with JoAnn.

"We'll need this when the pandemic is over and they let us out of jail," she said with a giggle, referring to the current locked-down life. She hoped to enable the residents in her community who were in their late seventies to 103 years old to get to know each other on a deeper level by sharing "who they were when." My eighty-six-year-old mother worked on establishing a committee, a logo, topics of conversation, and agendas. She censored inappropriate jokes and prompted questions over the course of the many months of lockdown. After getting the buzz started throughout her community and lining up speakers, Schmoozing with JoAnn was ready to launch. When the number of COVID-19 cases went down, the meetings began, but with limited capacity and in full social-distance style. Schmoozing with JoAnn was the perfect remedy for this isolated, often lonely population. May the schmoozing and the friendships continue for many years to come!

Rachel experienced another example of growth from uncertainty or trauma during the early weeks of COVID. On a sweltering morning in the last week of March 2020, she set up her office on the patio since all the "quiet spaces" inside our house were already occupied by the rest of our Quaranteam. I stepped outside to see if she wanted a smoothie since I was on food prep, and I knew by the screwed-up look of disbelief on her face that something upsetting had taken place.

Other professionals at her place of employment had already been furloughed or, even worse, fired. She had worked for the company for almost seven years and had done everything right, which had enabled her to climb the corporate ladder while the company experienced several transitions and layoffs. We called her the survivor as she continued to acquire

an education regarding all facets of the "business of the business." She worked hard, and she was rewarded with positive professional mobility.

But at this pivotal COVID-19 time, she was no longer needed. She had thought she was part of the strategic team that would keep the company afloat, but she was wrong, and it hurt every nerve in her body. As a young professional, her job not only supported her financially; it was her identity. She was proud of her accomplishments and cherished her relationships. She loved the fashion industry, and overall she loved her job.

After figuring out the definition of furlough and filing for unemployment—which took place online at 6:00 a.m. due to the unemployment department's inability to handle the overabundance of applicants—Rachel took a deep breath and tried to find purpose in her professional pause. She spent several days in shock, living in her sweatpants on the sofa, watching mindless television, and absorbing herself in social media. Other than the rent payment on her New York apartment, she had very few expenses, which helped her find peace with her pause. She committed several hours a day to searching for a new professional path, but the rest of her time was free—something she had never experienced as an adult. She was always able to enjoy and relax during vacations and days off, but this was different and magnified because she was home in her childhood comforts.

For me, this situation offered an opportunity to spend an unusual amount of time with my adult daughter so I could get to know her as the woman she had become.

During the pandemic, the term "dancing with my daughter" had a different meaning. Yes, we did exercise dance classes together on our balcony for hours at a time. We sweated like pigs and laughed like hyenas as we danced through the days, weeks, and months with great rhythm, respect, and enjoyment. Like girlfriends, we spent a ridiculous amount of time together gathering food, cooking, cleaning, watching shows, beautifying, laughing, loving, and learning. We discussed everything—we shared our guts, and we shared our clothes. We made delicious culinary creations together as we discussed the concerns and crises in our world.

I always knew she was smart, but now I realized she had grown and developed her intellect to become a mature and wise woman beyond her years. From the background, before she was furloughed, I had overheard her leading her team of professionals on Zoom with sophistication, acumen, and authentic kindness. I saw that she is compassionate yet cautious, generous but not foolish, and most importantly, really knows who she is and is wonderfully comfortable in her own skin.

Our mother-daughter magic solidified, and her voice became the loudest voice in my head rather than my voice in hers. COVID gave us the time to choreograph our movements together. We're not going to Broadway, and some days we do the clumsy dance, but overall, we have great rhythm and love. I hope to continue the beauty and fun of dancing with my daughter, literally and figuratively.

Within a few months, Rachel was called back to work. Our "pandemic pause" time together was extraordinary, but her ability to be resilient and evolve both professionally and personally was inspiring. She managed change with healthy emotion, gratitude, humor, and confidence, which were indicative of her ability to shepherd her way into the future. She didn't need me to be the mother who led her through life; she needed me to be the mother who just loved her.

Meanwhile, after week five of the "quarantine pause," our

son Brian began giving the community a "Hit of Happiness." During the first few weeks of COVID-19, Brian's brain was processing at high speed, looking for something to give him a sense of purpose and enable him to help others who were confused, anxious, curious, and in disbelief regarding the impact of the virus on all our lives. He created a website, Hitofhappiness.com, and wrote his first blog post, sharing his intentions with the world.

This blog was not meant to be about COVID-19. After this first post, I will try to shy away from mentioning coronavirus when possible. But this blog was also created partially because of the coronavirus. Everyone has been impacted in some way because of COVID-19. It could be financially, relationally, emotionally, spiritually, or all the above. Every day was becoming the same. Our social network is limited to our Quaranteams. Keeping busy and staying sane have become today's "floss" and "get 10,000 steps per day." So, as someone who is generally the ultimate optimist, I took a long, hard look at how I can make the most of this situation. It is only in recognizing our limitations that we can start to overcome them. We (or at least most of us) can't go find the cure to this virus ourselves; we can't pay everyone's rent who lives paycheck-to-paycheck and was just laid off; and we can't make sure there is enough PPE for all medical workers who are courageously working on the front lines. But at a micro level, we can all make a difference, whether that's donating to a food bank, delivering meals to the elderly, or Facetiming people who are alone—we all have something to give.

Since that first blog post, Brian has continued to give, sharing himself from the inside out. With intelligence and empathy, he supplements his knowledge of happiness with personal reflection. The science of happiness is not about always being happy with a shit-eating grin on our face; what allows us to feel real happiness is accepting and processing all emotions—both pain and pleasure.

Pre-pandemic, Brian, my friend Amy, and I took a year-long virtual course taught by Harvard professor Tal Ben-Shahar. I had heard Tal speak at a few events regarding the science of happiness and found a great deal of relatability in his wisdom. Always loving to learn, I signed up for the course with Amy, my "happiness friend."

Earlier, Amy had introduced me to the World Happiness Summit, an event I originally attended with hesitation only because the word *happiness* sounded so frivolous to me at the time. Much to my surprise, the event was fabulous, fulfilling, and fortuitous. It was three days filled with high-level presenters who provided insights about the importance of relationships, self-care, giving, spirituality, kindness, and purpose—everything that speaks to me in both my personal and professional life.

During one of my Facetime chats with my son Brian while he was working on a consulting job and traveling from coast to coast every week, I mentioned that I had attended the event and signed up for the science of happiness course. I had a feeling that his work-life balance was out of whack and that he might need a boost of happiness, so I told him about the class and offered to pay for it. Even though he wasn't certain he had time to do the work, he immediately said sure. As usual, loving doing anything with my children, I was thrilled that in his miniscule amount of spare time, we would be studying happiness together, even if we were in different time zones or continents, depending on where his work took him.

Who knew that a global pandemic would bring my global consultant back into my home where from his tiny workspace he would begin his Hit of Happiness (HoH) journey. When he introduced the name to our Quaranteam at dinner one night, my instant reaction was "Hit—that sounds like a hit of marijuana." With laughter and eye rolls, the family, including Kenny, let me know that I was being my wacky motherly self and that "hit" was relatable and relevant language.

Hit of Happiness now has thousands of followers who are happy to receive a weekly blog post, podcast episode, list of happiness habits, or weekly dose of wisdom. It took a pandemic for Brian to get his creative juices flowing, but they began overflowing at the right time. The world needs a "Hit of Happiness" now more than ever.

Millennials have had to learn to pause, pivot, and innovate. For many Boomers, too, this time gave us an opportunity to get off autopilot and push ourselves out of our comfort zones. My financially savvy friend Debbie shared with me a new challenge she took on during quarantine. With her adult son, she co-created the podcast "Bitcoin for Mom." It happened organically when she took an interest and asked her son Justin about bitcoin. A Millennial who is knowledgeable and passionate about bitcoin, Justin shared a lot of information. Even though Debbie was good at math and business, she recognized that there was a learning curve to understanding the technology and intricacies of cryptocurrency. Mother and son realized that their experience would probably resonate with many other Boomers and Millennials, and their goal was to simplify and teach about bitcoin on an accessible level. Debbie said doing this project and recording the podcasts together was fun, and she learned from working with her son that both generations need each other.

"They have knowledge we don't have, and we have knowledge they don't have," she said. "We think so differently."

Tom Vanderbilt, in *Beginners: The Joy and Transformative Power of Lifelong Learning*, emphasizes the importance of adults being open to learning new skills and embracing the enthusiasm of seeing new things as a beginner. With a beginner's mind, Vanderbilt explains, the ego dissolves, and the world becomes more interesting. It's also helpful to maintain a sense of purpose as we age. Author Meg Selig says that having a strong sense of purpose, whether taking care of grandchildren or a community cause, can lead to better health and longevity. As Boomers age, attitude and intention affect happiness.

Clearly, it is very important to keep growing and innovating. People are living longer now. In less than fifteen years, people aged sixty-five and up will outnumber those eighteen and under for the first time in US history. This major demographic shift presents a good opportunity for reevaluating our stereotypes and negative assumptions about getting older.

One of the blessings of aging is becoming a grandparent. During COVID, some families not only spent tremendous amounts of time with their adult children but also with their grandchildren. My dear friend Andrea shared with me that when the pandemic began, her daughter, son-in-law, and three-month-old grandson fled to Miami from their high-rise lifestyle in New York City. None of them realized that a year later they would still be living together.

"Our silver lining is the opportunity to be with our grandson every day," Andrea said. "My husband and I take care of him while our daughter and husband are working."

Their day-to-day responsibilities and professional commitments became the grandparents' day-to-day calendar of activities. They learned to establish boundaries and partnerships, which led to the organic occurrence of BooMillennial moments. Together, they experienced their grandson's "first everything"—smiles, crawling, walking, and running. They all felt his sleepless nights and teething trauma right along with the joy of his laughter. Will they all live under the same roof forever? Probably not, but their intergenerational living experience brought tremendous joy to their lives and to their ninety-year-old Grammy who came for weekly patio visits throughout the pandemic. Four generations were weathering the same tragic storm but in the lifeboat together—precious!

My friends Brad and Lauren refer to their pandemic pause time as "a blessing to have our kids and grandkids in our bubble." I remember thirty years ago when Lauren and I bonded following Hurricane Andrew. The storm caused us both to relocate, placing us in temporary housing not far from one another. Lauren and I connected while sharing stories of the destruction the hurricane brought into our lives. Now we were living another type of tragedy, but thankfully, three decades later, we were smarter and more aware of the tools we needed to get through the tough stuff.

Lauren and Brad escaped the virus by taking a few trips back and forth from Miami to the Berkshire Mountains of Massachusetts in their newly purchased recreational vehicle. That allowed them to travel with limited exposure to "the Germies," a term for COVID-19 that they learned from their four-year-old grandson. They spent time with their children and grandchildren, including their two new grandsons who were born during the pandemic, all while working, volunteering, and overseeing health care for their senior parents.

"Having the opportunity to live with our adult children and watch them interact and raise their own families plus being together as our family grows, has been the best bonus ever," Lauren told me.

My friend Meredith shared yet another story of the power of the pause sending adult children and grandchildren back home. We were both standing in line at the local market, socially distanced with masks on our faces, desperately wanting to hug because we were so happy to see each other. Meredith was my personal trainer for over twenty years, inspiring me with her positive energy and often serving as a confidant and therapist during our sweat sessions. She had snippets of wisdom that were always spot on.

When my children were young, she told me, "The best book you can give to your children is a passport. They'll learn more from traveling the world than from most of the books in the library." We have practiced those wise words with our children and have shared them with others. Many of us have had the opportunity to share wise words or simple organic wisdom back and forth with our Millennials during our pause time together.

Meredith summarized her BooMillennial experience beautifully. "I have found that our children became more friends than children. We love to be with each other but also lead our independent lives. It is our total pleasure to watch our children become parents, husbands, wives, and successful professionals. We also love the fact that they love to be with us!"

One afternoon in the spring of 2021 when a few of us were sitting outside at Starbucks, I heard a friend of mine say, "We lost a year." The sun was shining, the air was breezy, and we were all so grateful to be sitting and talking together, just like we used to—in person! Did we lose a year? I shook my head. "No, we didn't," I said. In fact, our "lost year" brought us many gains that we are just now beginning to see. The pandemic pause time with all its uncertainty and the steady monotony of days, weeks, and months of no planning was full of new insights and understanding.

14

The Journey Is the Destination

Growth Is the Accomplishment

March 2021

Laura

The COVID journey was a lesson in learning to live in uncertainty and embrace both the joy and sorrow that are inevitable in life. What will our new normal or destination look like? How will it impact us, our children, our parents, our colleagues, and our friends?

My family often jokes that our dog Louie is my favorite child, and they are probably right. My friend Diana dubbed Louie the "winner of COVID." Rain or shine, the dog was my motivation to get my butt to the park every morning and afternoon, and not surprisingly, I'd see the same familiar faces. Runners, a couple rollerblading, young mommies pushing their babies in strollers, and so many dog walkers like me were grateful to be outside doing something—anything that mattered.

One morning I took a different route on my walk with Louie. As if it were a mirage, I saw my yoga instructor, who

I had not seen since the start of the pandemic. "Is that really you?" I asked incredulously as I made my way across the field of dewy grass. "Yes!" she said with a beautiful smile. "Every Monday, Wednesday and Friday at 7:30 am, here I am." It must have been divine intervention. For the remaining weeks of lockdown, early morning yoga in the park became my most beloved ritual. A small but loyal and consistent community of grateful yogis gathered under the canopy of oak trees, laying our mats in a circle as we breathed, bent, and downward dogged our way through the days of COVID-19. In a cross-legged seated position with our palms placed at our hearts, we ended the class with gratitude and meaningful meditation. "May your day be blessed with peace, love, light and much joy. Namaste."

I was grateful to be with people. The pandemic made me realize how much I need people. I've always been unafraid to say hello to a stranger or give someone a compliment. If I'm waiting in line at a store, I invariably find a way to make polite conversation with the person standing next to me.

"You don't always have to be that person," Emily has often said to me. Why have I always felt the need to tell the girl wearing the yellow shirt, "You look beautiful, and I love that color!" I'm not sure. Why do I whisper reassuringly to the mother deep in negotiations with her toddler who is having a meltdown in the Starbucks line at the airport, "Don't worry, he'll grow out of it." Emily was probably right, but personal connection has always been so important to me.

Back from the park, I put Louie's leash in the drawer, and Emily motioned to me from the patio. Two of her friends from New York were visiting, enjoying the weather in Miami. "Come sit with us, Mommy," Emily said.

"Mommy" is code for "I need love," my very best skill

set. And when it is said in front of her friends, it means I can pour it on even thicker. I jumped at the opportunity, plopping down in the Adirondack chair. I was grateful that they wanted me to hang out with them.

"How was the park?" one of the girls asked.

"It was beautiful," I said. "But I've got to tell you, I see so many people walking around with AirPods in their ears and their faces in their phones that I'm worried, girls." I tried not to sound too much like a Debbie downer. "With all the technology, do you guys actually know how to connect and relate to each other?"

For a split second I thought my daughter might actually ask me to go back in the house. But instead, the three young women took the bait and dove right in. What ensued was one of the most thoughtful, intelligent, and reassuring conversations I'd had in a long time. We talked about politics, abortion rights, the environment, and women in the new remote working world. Sharp, smart, and self-aware, these were three fabulous young women, well-educated and empowered. Despite the pandemic that had upended their lives, a job market in flux, and the challenges that lay ahead, they were strong, grounded, and prepared to take on the world. It was their time. That much was clear.

"You girls are going to change this world," I said, again feeling a tear welling up behind my sunglasses. "And you're going to need to because my generation has really left it in a crappy place."

It will be interesting to see where and how these women make their mark. In their early twenties, they seemed so much more impressive than I remember myself at that age. Every generation hopes to leave the world better for the next generation that follows. This time of pause made all of us examine our choices. For me, it put a magnifying glass on my parenting, shining the spotlight for me to share in my kids' greatest accomplishments and illuminate my insecurities.

Out of my routine and hunkered down inside with my adult children, I was able to see everything Dan and I did well in raising them. I am deeply proud of their character and integrity. We were also able to see all the flaws and imperfections, as well as our own regrets up close and personal, right there in living color. Good or bad, "we left it all out on the field," as Dan has always said. But even so, no matter how much effort we put into parenting our kids, we have no answers for how to navigate the world we are living in today, and that is difficult to accept. One thing I know for sure, I am lucky to be their mom.

I walked back into the house, and upstairs Jacob and Steph were nestled on the couch, both looking intently at Jacob's laptop.

"What are you guys reading?" I asked my son and daughter-in-law.

"We're planning a trip to Italy," Jacob said with a wide grin.

"Italy! Is the pandemic over? Is Italy even open for international travel yet?" I asked, already running through nervous scenarios of my children getting COVID and being forced to quarantine abroad. On the other hand, I couldn't think of a country I'd rather be stranded in. A little pasta and Chianti sounded pretty good.

"I have a couple weeks before the new job starts," Jacob explained. "We want to get away, and this is the perfect time."

"Sounds fabulous," I said as I walked into the kitchen, wondering to myself whether these two adorable, almost-thirty-somethings were thinking about starting a family. Was I ready to become a grandmother? Me? Grandmothers are old. I wasn't *that* old yet. On the other hand, I couldn't think of anything I'd rather be doing than holding a little baby. Maybe I was getting ahead of myself. Maybe they just wanted to take a trip together, but if a mother's instinct counted for anything, mine was usually pretty accurate. Were they ready to become parents? Is anyone ever ready?

Being a mom and helping children grow into good human beings is not for the faint of heart. Motherhood is the most challenging, gratifying, all-consuming, and meaningful journey of a lifetime.

I appreciated being asked to join the conversation with Emily and her friends on the patio. I adored that Jacob and Steph wanted to travel and see the world. Obviously, it's not my business if they are ready to start a family. Our children are the new generation of parents, professionals, and leaders. They will change the world, travel the world, and enjoy their lives. Yet they are different than we are—thank goodness.

March 23, 2021

And just like that, Andrew's last day at home arrived. An entire year had gone by, and now my middle child was returning to New York. In some ways, it felt like an eternity, and at the same time it seemed like he had arrived just a minute ago.

All the little moments—was I present for it all? Did I pay attention? I appreciated the afternoon breaks when we talked together. I liked his kind way of asking most evenings, "Can I help you with anything?"—whether he meant it or not. The little quirky traditions we established will now live on in my memory.

"Do you want another cup of coffee?" I asked him every afternoon around 1:30 or 2:00. At the beginning of COVID, he would never have had coffee in the afternoon, but by the end of the year, he had crossed over to the dark side and was, like me, a two-plus-cup-a-day person.

I had come to love our peanut butter and jelly sandwiches with a side of Doritos. I often said, "I'm fifty-six; I shouldn't be eating like I'm twenty-six." But in retrospect, those were our best bonding meals, and I wouldn't change a thing. We also enjoyed our Sunday night Indian food takeout while streaming a new series on TV.

Dan would also miss his son tremendously—their Friday morning golf games, the Saturday morning bike rides. It was a year full of modified sporting events. It seemed odd that Andrew was leaving during March Madness. Shouldn't we all just be sitting on the couch watching basketball together?

There were moments throughout the year when time seemed to stand still. All I wanted was some type of forward movement, anything at all. Now suddenly, I was already feeling that familiar maternal pang that I still feel whenever one of my kids leaves, even though they are now all adults. It's a juxtaposition of pride, gratitude, and relief that they are grown, independent, capable adults living their own lives, along with the recognition that we would soon be returning to our empty nest.

When the kids were little, I loved planning. I planned what I was going to put in their lunchboxes, what activities and teams they would play on, what vacations we would take. Living in the pandemic taught us to live life making no plans—and just "be."

I sat on Andrew's bed downstairs, watching him as he packed his clothes in his suitcase. "It's funny how different things can look in hindsight," Andrew said. "I know, I know," he continued, "the age-old saying, 'hindsight is twenty-twenty,' but as it was happening, waking up each morning and walking upstairs in my pajamas to sit at the dining room table (my makeshift office) felt unbelievably monotonous. It felt like I was Bill Murray in the movie *Groundhog Day*, just waiting and waiting and waiting for something (anything) to feel new or different. And it never did. *Never*. Not once. But I know I'm not alone here."

Andrew was right. In some way or another for the last year or so, everyone's life resembled this debilitatingly repetitive existence. But sometimes it's only when you are removed from something long enough or far enough that you can begin to see its real value.

"In some ways," Andrew continued, "I'm almost nostalgic for the simplicity of the pandemic experience. The big existential questions like 'What do you want to do with your life?' were suddenly replaced with far less significant ones like 'Do I want Cool Ranch or Sweet Chili Doritos with my sandwich for lunch today?'" Andrew chuckled.

I watched Andrew as he folded his T-shirts with military-like precision and placed them neatly in his suitcase. He continued to share reflections from his year back home, remembering feeling relieved that "there was nobody on some unforgettable international excursion, nobody asking you what your plans were for the weekend, and nothing too special to look forward to." Instead, Andrew said that for the first time in his life, watching too much TV or focusing on something small like learning how to make challah was more than acceptable—it was exactly what he needed.

"I needed to regain a sense of simplicity, and I needed 552 conversations with my parents about the state of our world, what we've seen, learned, and felt," Andrew said. "I needed all the time that came with those conversations to simply process it all."

I thought about all the conversations I had with Andrew during this time and all the things I learned from him. I remembered one afternoon when I came back from Walgreens, frustrated about something. As I repeated the story to Andrew, it was my son who helped me gain a new perspective, instructing me to be more patient and sensitive.

"Mom, people are really struggling," he said. "If you can't make it better, just keep your mouth shut," he cautioned me. "You may not be able to make it better, but you can at least be nice." Those wise words I continue to remember in my daily interactions.

In hindsight, Andrew said he never would have imagined that a year of living at home at twenty-six years old with his parents and siblings would have such a positive impact. He was grateful for the time to recenter, reground, and pause to ask himself the questions he needed to ask at this time in his life.

Heading back to New York, my son was a different person than he was when he came home a year before. Andrew was more mature, more thoughtful, and more insightful. And with my newfound sense of self-restraint, I was no longer that mother who barraged him with nonsensical questions that I knew he did not want to answer.

After our BooMillennial year together, I knew that, in his words, he would "figure it out." While I know that living with his parents was not easy, he got through it, and he was now ready to go, emerging from our time together as a stronger, steadier, more confident version of himself. Certainly, he had developed an even better sense of humor.

It was a year of growth. We were able to provide Andrew with stability and a place to catch his breath in order to process this time of uncertainty. We gave him an abundance of love and attention and the space he needed. Like a personal pit crew, we fixed him up, and now he was getting back out there on the road again, venturing out on his own journey.

15

Bonus Time with Our Boys

Life Is Full of Surprises

April 2021

Adrian

Running into the kitchen with his laptop open, Brian said enthusiastically, "Mom, look at this Airbnb. It's simple and spacious enough so the Koffsky crew can stay with us at Lake Placid. It's perfect!"

"Yes, it looks spacious, that's for sure," I responded without really looking at the pictures as I poured the balsamic glaze on top of the roasting Brussels sprouts. "What's the cancellation policy?" I asked, still not believing that this Ironman endeavor was really going to happen. It just felt so unfathomable to me. I quickly shifted focus, letting my family know that dinner was ready and hoping that the conversation at the table would be about anything other than the Ironman. It scared me like a family of rabid raccoons breaking into my house in the middle of the night.

Brian sat at the dinner table rubbing his eyes with his fists just like he did as a baby, signaling that he was tired. Of course he was tired. He had started his day at 5:30 a.m. to meet his triathlon training team for a swim in the ocean, followed by an endurance bike ride and a sprinted run. This was usually followed by a big bowl of oatmeal and a shower before kicking off his first work Zoom meeting of the day.

His professional day was filled with team meetings, connectivity chats, coaching sessions, science of happiness check-ins, and a few moments of personal meditation. Usually around 1:00 p.m. he popped out of his office-bedroom for a lunch break where he consumed mostly greens and grains, often prepared by his personal chef—me—while taking the time for a few deep breaths.

Brian's afternoon usually mimicked his morning with slight variations, and by 6:00 p.m., he took a quick walk and talk, usually on Facetime with his friends regarding "how to change the world" or something profound. Dinner, again prepared by me, was usually served by 7:00 p.m. Brian preferred at least two hours to digest his food before going to sleep. Dinner was usually full of active conversation regarding Brian's day or the upcoming day's routine. Sometimes we'd chat about world events, the stock market, golf tee times for the weekend, or other top-of-mind topics. On occasion during dinner, we listened to one of the Path to Happiness sessions he had presented to 2,000 participants at his place of employment or partook in a cousins Zoom to stay up-to-date on everyone's lives.

At about 7:48 p.m., the rubbing of the fatigued eyes began, and Brian would retire to his bedroom-office to finish his work, write the weekly Hit of Happiness, and read some form of motivational or inspirational literature for at least thirty minutes before slumbering, usually by 9:00 p.m. That enabled him to attempt to get much-needed REM sleep so he could wake up the following morning and do it all over again.

By the way, we knew all about Brian's sleep and how it impacted his routine, since he always wore a WHOOP on his wrist that measured his vitals, including calories burned, how his sleep serviced his bodily needs, and the color of his underwear—just kidding! So of course he was freakin' tired. I'm tired just sharing his story.

Due to the pandemic, Brian had been our "roommate" for the best part of a year, and I will begin by revealing that we are all fully aware that a twenty-seven-year-old man who is independent and employed should not be living with his parents. Having said that, we called this "bonus time" with our boy. Bonus time with Brian was an amazing gift on many levels.

Brian has an innate kindness that has served him well. When he was a toddler, strangers would touch his red hair at the grocery store and ask me if it was real. *Really?* I thought to myself. *Would I color my child's hair?* Brian would smile, loving the attention. Having an older sister, Rachel, who adored him and always communicated with him with authority and leadership, gave him the best playmate ever. He loved her and happily followed her lead. Brian was my "go with the flow" guy.

When Brian graduated from high school and went off to the University of Florida's business school with plans to acquire an accounting degree, Rachel was finishing her last year at the same university. That gave them the opportunity to experience the Florida Gator nation together and create absurdly fun memories. Many stories of their time together during both high school and college were shared with us over our COVID-era dinner table. The ridiculousness of their frolics would make for great entertainment streaming on Netflix or HBO Max. They are a couple of characters—good characters who had great big fun!

The kids had also been very glad to spend some of their vacation time with us on our travels. Of course, it was incentivized by the fact that they knew it was our pleasure to take care of all their travel expenses. We were mindful of the good advice offered by our dear friends Michele and Robert, who have older children, when our kids were entering their teen years: "Keep your time together fun, and they will always want to be with you." Who knew that one day they would flee home to us to outrun the coronavirus? Were we that much fun?

During this time with our son, we evolved with him. As the frontal lobe of his brain closed, our neural pathways got deeper. We felt his professional frustrations and success, his innovative and entrepreneurial yearnings, and his daily exercise rituals. Did we understand them during week seven of the pandemic? No, not at all. In our eyes, he was accomplished and living his life with precision and at a nice steady pace. But by week fifty-two, we understood his desires and dreams. We had deep, daily, face-to-face communication—something Kenny and I did not have with our own parents as adults because we never lived with them after the age of eighteen when we left for college.

Having had the opportunity to really know and understand our son Brian, we became aligned with his dreams and desires. We understood his fatigue when he rubbed his tired eyes at the dinner table, and we eagerly awaited his weekly Hit of Happiness. The front-row seat into his life as an amazing young man was a gift we will treasure forever. But as for this Ironman endeavor, until we saw him and his good friend Andrew cross the finish line in vertical positions, we just didn't get it!

Laura and I often reflect on our sons' Ironman adventure. We also talk often about how quickly the years have flown. From the days of walking the boys into preschool together to becoming professional partners in Good Work Miami, LLC, to many years of a beautiful and easy friendship, we never expected to live through a year that would culminate with our standing at the finish line in Lake Placid, New York, as we became IronMoms together.

Our plane landed in Albany, New York. "Hi, Brian, we just landed in Albany. Do you need any groceries?" I quickly typed the list into my phone. "How's the Airbnb?"

"It's fine," he replied. "It's everything we need." I sighed with relief, not yet knowing that in a few hours after I inspected the place, I would be calling Laura, who was still at her mother-in-law's house in Connecticut, with a request that she bring shower shoes, towels, pillowcases, and Lysol.

Our entire cast of characters—our two families—convened in Lake Placid at our five-bedroom, four-bathroom, perfectly located lakeside accommodations on Main Street above Ben and Jerry's. We humorously called it "the Dumpaporium," because it was a dump, decorated in circa 1969 décor. But it met our humble needs during a weekend of letting go of our motherly neuroses, laughing *a lot*, and finding so much goodness in two sons who were going to make a remarkable accomplishment.

We prepared their pre-race cuisine. My Brian dined on salmon and spinach salad sprinkled with cashews for that extra crunch and fat. Andrew's girlfriend prepared him some pasta Bolognese with expert culinary skills and limited cooking utensils. At the kitchen table, Brian spread almond butter and organic jelly on Dave's bread, preparing eight sandwiches for race day. He strategically planned how many he could zip into his biking shirt.

"Andrew, why aren't you making sandwiches like Brian?" Laura asked her son. She was concerned. "What are you going to eat during the race?"

Although Andrew tried to explain that he and Brian had both done in-depth research and each made their own independent plans for the race, I could see Laura's anxiety growing with each sandwich Brian produced.

"Andrew, really, you need to eat," Laura insisted. "You need fuel. You can't go all day without food."

"I've got it, Mom. Please stop worrying!" Andrew said with annoyance.

The boys presented us with yellow sticky notes stating their Ironman rules—for us. Can you imagine? They had rules for us, their loving mothers, who had traveled a great distance to cheer them on through their self-induced extremely arduous day. Andrew read aloud the number-one rule: *No worrying!* "We've worked hard to train for this race," he said, "and we want to accomplish this. We don't need your worry to derail us. We need you to dig in and support us."

Our boys knew us way too well, but did they really think that a sticky note would be the miracle cure for our motherly crazies?

"Relax. Trust us. We've got this figured out," they said nearly in unison.

Brian often reminded us that he has always figured things out over the course of his young adult life. Whether it was how to complete a Master's degree and pass the CPA exam at the same time, how to train to become an Ironman while working full time, how to launch Hit of Happiness into the world and get accepted to a very fine entrepreneurial MBA program—he has total ownership of his life and will figure out how to solve any problems that arise. It was time for these two moms to figure out how to disengage our overly devoted neurotic parenting genes and let the young men fly.

"I see him!" Rachel screamed as Brian made his way out of the water, already removing his wet suit as he emerged with a smile. "Where's Andrew?" I asked uneasily. Why weren't they together? I was always happy when they stayed together during their younger days. Why weren't they together now?

"Andrew finished his swim eight minutes ago. He's already in the transition area," Dan said, walking fast hoping to see him before he got on his bike.

Andrew's body language radiated "serious but happy" as he quickly changed into his biking gear, checking and rechecking that he had everything he needed for success. Brian's transition went smoothly, and both boys rocked with confidence as they set off on their bike rides. We rocked with nausea and the need for more coffee to get us through the hours ahead. Seven hours on a bicycle, up and down hills, dealing with funky weather, screaming fans and fears—*our* fears. They rode the pavement while our intestines felt like they were rupturing. We had a few sneak-a-peek spots where we cheered them on, so happy to see them in an upright position. At the top of one hill, Laura spotted my son Brian, and tears came to her eyes as she saw him thanking the fans for their cheers and encouragement. "He looks fantastic!" she beamed at me as she came running back to the place on the curb where we were all standing. "He's actually waving and thanking the spectators." Laura and Brian had a special connection—they were born on the same month and day, February 20, thirty years apart. They both share the gift of innate kindness and gratitude that their astrological genes produced.

We screamed, celebrated, and sighed with intense relief as both boys dismounted their bikes with wobbly legs, soaked in sweat but somehow able to muster up a smile for the fans and their mothers while they transitioned into running attire for the last leg of their extraordinary athletic journey. They had only 26.2 miles to run to finish their endeavor. Only 26.2 miles to go!

Andrew and Brian took off with confidence, knowing they would finish the race even if they had to crawl to the finish line. Their relief was apparent by the levity of their demeanor as they moved their bodies for many hours toward the enchanted ending of their miraculous accomplishment. There we were at the finish line after fourteen hours of their intense athleticism and our intense neuroticism. We were all filled with indescribable emotions as our eyes welled up with tears as we gave our Ironman boys salty, sweaty hugs and kisses. We realized then that yes, they could "figure it out."

We called the grandparents and shouted that Brian and Andrew had done it! They had accomplished the Ironman. Some of our nearest and dearest had been following Andrew and Brian on the Ironman app and sent congratulatory texts. Our phones blew up with Facetimes and calls.

"This was the greatest day ever!" I said to my cousins Julie and Stuart.

"You dreaded and doubted this day so much," Julie responded. "Just look how much you've evolved!"

Becoming an Ironman is only partially about the physical training. Equally important is the mental preparation and exertion. It is about reframing your thoughts, changing your habits, relinquishing control, and having commitment, flexibility, optimism, some fears, and faith. It is about evolving the total being—mind, body, and spirit—to accomplish the mission.

"Andrew Koffsky, you're an Ironman," Brian chanted the morning after. Andrew had just gingerly walked into the kitchen of the Dumpaporium in his boxers and his full-on "sleepy face," which we all remember from his childhood days.

Andrew returned the chant to Brian. "And Brian Dubow, you're an Ironman! We did it, Bro. We actually did it. A memory for the books—one and done?" Andrew asked.

Brian smiled, and for a moment we stopped breathing, waiting for Brian's answer. "Probably not one and done, but we can chill today! Where should we go to breakfast?"

Off to the diner we went where everyone did some carb replenishing. These guys knew what they were doing and how they were doing it. And boy, did they do it, crossing the finish line of a lifetime.

Just like Andrew and Brian, we had all evolved as we neared the ever-changing finish line of the pandemic. We survived and thrived, and look at how much we accomplished. We found our comfortable normal, understanding that the future will inevitably bring challenges for which we will now be better equipped to meet with flexibility, grit, and less neurosis.

16

Passing the Torch

Let the Next Generation Lead

W e texted each other at 8:13 a.m. on May 19, 2023, con-
firming that we were both watching the *Today* show
segment about the ongoing return of adult children to their
parents' homes. Some parents were now charging their adult
children rent each month, hoping to instill a sense of responsibility and accountability as their kids moved into adulthood. Some
parents accepted the rental income happily, while others saved
it for their child renter to use when they were ready to launch.

As we all know, 2020 had changed the housing landscape,
bringing both Millennials and Gen Z-ers back into their parents' homes at the highest rate in decades. According to the
US Pew report, one out of four young adults returned home
that year. In 2023, young adults are still boomeranging back
into their parents' homes in order to save money and continue to simmer into maturity. There is also a trend for Baby
Boomers to move in with their children while they as parents
are still young enough to be helpful and relevant. This new
collective cohabitation opens the opportunity for new intergenerational synergy and the potential for living differently
with a newfound level of respect and appreciation.

We have changed significantly since the pandemic arrived on our doorsteps in March 2020 and forced us to face the many challenges and emotions, whether they were affecting our world or ourselves and our families. We paused, pivoted, repurposed, reflected, and purchased more essential items and stretchy clothing than ever before. The impossible became the possible, the unexpected happened, control was relinquished, and anxiety was heightened. We connected, communicated differently, and cared for one another with compassion and kindness.

We learned a lot about a lot of things we never knew. We were given the opportunity to gain new perspectives regarding the generations that came before us. We Baby Boomers joined our Millennial children to become BooMillennials. We developed deep and insightful relationships with this generation of amazing young people we have raised, and we realized the importance of collaboratively working together to take on the many challenges in our world. We gained a greater understanding of what their vision is for the future, and we realized that the time is now for them to take the lead. While we will always be there with our support and love—and, when asked, with our wisdom—this time has compelled us to reexamine and recalibrate our own roles as parents and maturing professionals and leaders.

We have opened our minds and hearts while realizing that we need to shut up, release, encourage, love, listen, and laugh all at the same time. We are the change-makers. For healthy evolution to take place from generation to generation, needs must be identified, appreciated, and allowed to unfold. Succession is the key to success in both the family unit and organizations.

Our parents' generation had nothing, and they exceeded their expectations. How quickly our generation evolved from the simplicity of catching fireflies in the backyard to expecting instant gratification with abundance of choice and a widening gap of inequity and dissatisfaction in today's world. Have we prepared the next generation to make lemonade out of all this?

Organizations will not be sustainable if outreach to younger generations is not an ongoing strategy. We need to know when to push our chairs back from the decision-making table, take a seat on the side, and allow room for the next team of leaders to pull their chairs to the head of the table and lay out their own bold, new vision—one that will lead us all into the future.

We found our North Star, our personal mission statement, in writing this book, and we will be forever grateful for our time together. We have loved sharing our memoir and the stories of others during the most unique time in our lives. But enough of us, we are passing the torch and the mic to the next generation—our future!

June 14, 2023

Brian

Thanks to the pandemic, Andrew and I have both pivoted in new directions, tried new professions, and experienced living in new cities. Four days after the Ironman, I moved to Los Angeles to begin my MBA studies at the UCLA Anderson School of Management. I've spent the last two years reflecting on who I am and what impact I want to make on the world while focusing my studies on entrepreneurship and leadership development.

My life went from very small during quarantine to very big quickly since my MBA presented me with amazing academics, sent me on trips around the world, and put me in conversations with extremely accomplished and interesting people.

At times, I wish my life was still as simple as those first few months of COVID, but now, as a recent MBA grad, I'm filled with excitement and optimism for what is to come. My focus is now fully devoted to Hit of Happiness where I coach, consult, and lead workshops and trainings in support of individual and corporate well-being and happiness. My true goal with Hit of Happiness is to help people feel alive and remind them that happiness is a choice!

Andrew and I still have our weekly catchup calls to check in on what crazy ideas we're considering now and what's keeping us awake at night. Andrew spent the past year completing a Master's degree in real estate at Columbia University in New York City. He then returned to Miami to provide new leadership for his dad's established real estate and construction business. They are living the succession dream.

I texted Andrew today to ask him if he was prouder of being an Ironman or of acquiring a Master's degree from Columbia University. Without any hesitation, he responded, "Ironman!" I couldn't agree more. While we are both grateful for our graduate school educations and experiences, our shared Ironman journey will be imprinted on our minds forever, a lasting highlight on our life résumés.

The Ironman taught us that we can do anything we put our minds to. Sure, we proved that physically, but it also holds true when it comes to professional, intellectual, and relational goals. We hope to find another extreme athletic endeavor to pursue when time permits, knowing that our mothers' neurological systems have evolved to a place of less neurosis—not!

We realize it is very possible that neither of us would have become an Ironman at this age or had the privilege to get to know ourselves better and reboot our life trajectories without COVID-19. The pause of the pandemic allowed us to return home, whether we wanted to or not, and have the opportunity to connect, breathe, and spend meaningful quality time with our families.

As for our siblings, my sister Rachel continues to shine in her profession while living her best life in Miami. Andrew's sister Emily is now a working professional in New York City, enjoying every opportunity the Big Apple offers. Andrew's brother Jacob and his wife Steph are working more while sleeping less as the proud parents of a one-year-old baby girl we affectionately call "Princess Happiness." We are grateful to know we can count on each other as our lives post-COVID continue to evolve.

To our parents, thank you for all you've done. Thanks for loving us, thanks for guiding us, and thanks for always being there for us. Our relationships have reached an entirely new level. There is a newfound mutual respect and understanding that comes from being on the front lines and seeing how we live our lives. We know exactly what makes you tick, we know what tics are never going to change, and we are good with that—actually, we like that. We are so grateful for all you've done for us. That said, if you want to continue being there for us, we have a hard truth for you. Step aside.

It's time to test how well you really did, and the only way to do that is to let us lead our lives. Let us make our own decisions. Even if we make mistakes, we will learn from them. Let us define what a happy and successful life looks like for ourselves. Let us be the change we want to see in the world. And don't worry. The more space you give us, the more we will ask for your input.

Your job from here on is to take care of yourselves. Exercise daily, eat healthy, and keep your minds stimulated so you can continue to bestow your wisdom not only on us but on our kids, the next generation who will be lucky enough to also have the privilege of learning from the Baby Boomers.

Good Work

More Stories of Finding Sweetness Amidst the Sourest of Times

July 2023

Adrian and Laura

When the world was at a standstill and the unknown seemed overwhelming, people somehow stepped up and gave of themselves for a greater good. Families and communities came together like never before, adapting in real time and finding solutions to the real-life challenges facing our world.

Many of us emerged better than when the pandemic began. We shed a lot the stuff about ourselves and our lives that we didn't like. The time of pause helped us reinforce our values and gave us the confidence to know that no matter what lies ahead, we can rely on ourselves to overcome difficult things. We gained the perspective to know that we must value our days and spend them meaningfully. We found clarity in the importance of empowering, mentoring, and listening to the next generation—including those who lived under our roofs—while appreciating and continuing to learn from the wisdom of the generations that came before us. Quite often it is in sharing some of life's sourest moments that we find the sweetest moments.

The Dignity of the Individual

Marcia, who retired after a long career in both for-profit and nonprofit marketing communications, said her avocation was always fiber arts. She recalled how she had serendipitously walked by the SAORI ArtsNYC storefront on the way to her apartment one day before the pandemic. Now called Intertwine Arts, the story is a beautiful one. A healing art form, it was created in Japan by Misao Jo in the late 1960s. A homemaker who started to weave when she was fifty-seven, Misao was surprised when a mistake in her first piece produced an unexpected beauty. She began to develop a weaving method that embraced imperfections and spontaneity, a timeless lesson that can resonate for anyone from any generation. The word *Saori* is a combination of the Zen term *sai*, which means "the dignity of the individual," and the Japanese word *ori*, which means "weaving."

Marcia enrolled in some of the circle weaving workshops, and then came the lockdown. With her husband Sam also retired and needing her care, Marcia knew this was her opportunity to pursue something she had always wanted to try. She got a loom and began to explore weaving. Finding it relaxing and cathartic, Marcia became passionate about this healing art form. Bringing her communication and marketing skills, Marcia helped Intertwine get into hospitals, which provided a creative outlet for families while their loved ones received chemotherapy and other treatments.

She helped execute a turn-key program that offered instruction on weaving, with the idea that parents and kids stuck at home together could use household items such as paper plates and craft items for weaving. Intertwine also supports the needs of the mentally and physically challenged population. Since her initial involvement, Marcia has been able to help the organization secure grants, hire a professional staff, and grow and scale Intertwine in its mission. Among the many things she has learned, Marcia said, "I don't want to waste time; it's too precious."

Volunteers and Vaccines

During COVID, volunteers had significant impacts. Our dear friend Julie worked tirelessly setting up vaccine appointments, and her team of volunteers was quite incredible. Julie and Laura have been friends since they were little girls, and Julie has always been one of the most positive people we know. Wise and caring, she is a problem-solver at her core. She and a small group of women mobilized and motivated each other to bring meaning and purpose to those otherwise long COVID days.

"We realized quite quickly that our work would be transformational for our community," Julie said. "We set our alarms and worked together day and night to procure as many appointments as we could. It was inspirational and magical. Together we secured over 5,000 vaccines for the greater community."

Our friends Monica and Tammi worked with local hospitals to help schedule the elderly and others in their community who were not technologically savvy and needed assistance. Born in Mexico, Monica said she empathized with people who had a language barrier since the forms and information necessary to register were complicated. Monica's work began organically through word of mouth when she helped one of her friends. Suddenly she found herself immersed, waking up early every day and helping as many people as she could. "I felt I had to give back and try to help wherever I could," Monica said.

Our friend Alisa told us about her super-senior friend Esther to whom she has provided physical and emotional support for more than eight years. Alisa became like family to Esther, and it was agonizing to be unable to care for her when the pandemic began. Simultaneously from a geographical distance, Alisa was also managing her ninety-year-old mother's health concerns during lockdown. Her mother's loneliness became magnified and painful for Alisa and her loved ones. People need people, and the lack of connection led to deterioration, depression, and physical and emotional challenges.

Awakening into Action

Susan, a friend of Laura's for more than thirty-five years, said that 2020 was a transformative time for her as she evolved from a corporate to a community leader. An advertising professional who worked in New York City for more than thirty-five years, Susan is also a successful entrepreneur, acquiring and renovating houses in the Hamptons over the years and renting them throughout the summer seasons.

With lockdown and all the New Yorkers flocking to the suburbs, demand for rental properties soared. Susan suddenly found herself phasing out of advertising and consulting work and focusing on her houses, a business that had become quite lucrative. She also moved out of the city and found herself living for the first time as a full-time resident in one of her properties in the Sag Harbor community. It provided a less frenetic pace with time and skills to give back.

We spoke as she was sitting on the train commuting back to the Hamptons. She reflected on how keenly she felt all the pain and loss in the world, as well as the issues of inequity and divisiveness. "I felt so privileged, and I felt non-participatory. I had to do something," she said. What was initially a volunteer role in an initiative for a food pantry grew into a much bigger operational role where she found herself interfacing with various constituencies and building bridges in the community.

"Seeing the disparity in the community is indicative that we need to be doing better, and there's a place and a need for everyone to help," Susan said. With experience mentoring Millennials in her workplace, she found herself helping create a collaborative environment at the food pantry so everyone involved felt important. She facilitated conversations that encouraged different points of view and empowered the next generation to lead.

"There's been tremendous suffering and sadness, but in some ways, like 9/11, this time was a gift from God," Susan said. "This was an opportunity to reset and advance, to find our values, focus on humanity and civility, and figure out what's important."

Education and Innovation

Our friend Nancy said it was Andrew who inspired her volunteer involvement with Teach for America (TFA). After college, Andrew took a position as a teacher in a TFA charter school, and Nancy said it was through him that she first learned about the need to assist teachers in the classroom. She had felt fortunate to be able to put her two sons through private school. She knew the value of education, and with both of them in college, she had time to give and wanted to use it in a meaningful way. Assigned to a first-grade classroom with a friend, they formed relationships with the children while teaching reading, helping with math problems, and facilitating whatever needed to be done to support the students' learning.

During the pandemic, when schools closed, Nancy said

the virtual format brought many challenges to the surface. She wanted to be helpful in any way she could and began one-on-one tutoring with a student two mornings a week. While she was used to a loud and boisterous classroom environment, the individual reading instruction she provided truly made a difference.

"It's hard not to see the brokenness of the system," Nancy said. "But the children all love the extra attention, and I was so happy to be able to give it. This time has opened everyone's eyes to the inequity and needs in our world."

Lisa, a first-grade teacher, told us that the COVID period taught her to be more patient and tolerant. A teacher for almost twenty years, she saw her world shift overnight from an in-person classroom to virtual instruction. She had to switch gears quickly and adapt in real time to read and respond to the emotions of her six-year-old students and their parents who were also quickly getting up to speed on the new technology and new ways of doing things from home. As head of her department, she also found herself in the challenging position of needing to be somewhat of a cheerleader, staying encouraging and energetic and motivating her team of fellow teachers. All of them were readjusting lesson plans and spending several hours each day responding to emails and returning phone calls to concerned parents. Like all teachers, they were also living their own "real" lives.

Lisa said the commitment she felt to her students is what gave her the energy to get up every morning and greet the day, knowing there would be moments of frustration but also great strides and growth. A competitive runner throughout her life, Lisa has always believed that people are more capable than they realize.

"It is amazing to see how my kids adapted," Lisa said with pride. "With a positive attitude, people rise to a challenge."

It's a Ride, Not a Race

Setting a goal and seeing it through is what initially inspired our friend Belinda to enter a seven-day, 640-mile bike ride down the coast of California in support of the Challenged Athletes Foundation.

"It is a ride, not a race!" she kept saying as she set aside the necessary hours to train and prepare leading up to the event. "Apparently, riding along the coast is a 'bucket list' item for many people," she said, laughing as she explained that she and her husband, both endurance athletes, were drawn to support the cause of riding alongside truly inspirational, challenged athletes with incomparable grit and determination.

The riders came from all over the United States, some having lost limbs when serving our country or because of accidents. Others had limbs missing at birth or had lost them due to disease. All of them came to the ride with a will to challenge themselves. And they inspired every person who rode for them. Belinda and her husband raised more than $50,000 from friends and colleagues for those who benefit from the Challenged Athletes Foundation.

Belinda said she treasures the memories—the spectacular setting, the California sunshine, the cold early mornings, the wind, and her sore body at the end of each day. Most of all, she cherishes the gift of riding alongside the special human beings who refused to allow their disabilities to disable them, challenging themselves to live meaningful lives through sport.

"If You Have a Lot on Your Plate, Get a Platter"

Unspoken angels—that's what some people walking in this world are. They are true angels inspiring us to be our best selves.

Throughout the Dallas community, Amy is known as one of those special souls. Anyone who knows her knows that she is a knitter. In the beginning of the quarantine, her two sons returned home from college. Amy and her family played many rounds of Scrabble and assembled dozens of jigsaw puzzles until, much to her surprise, her sons asked her to teach them to knit.

In the beginning of the pandemic when people were paralyzed with fear, Amy said knitting presented a great distraction. So she taught her sons to knit, and she was blown away by how they got into it. The first project they took on was knitting baby hats. They knitted 156 of them and delivered them to the hospital in Dallas for the new babies born in this crazy, historic time.

"I've always felt that when you feel so helpless, doing for others is the best thing to do," Amy said.

Amy has always been a caring person, and her mother and mother-in-law were her models. If her mother ever saw a need, she told a few people, and soon a committee was formed to solve the problem. In Amy's recollection, that is how things always got done.

Amy is inspired by her mother-in-law's words, "If you have a lot on your plate, get a platter." She learned that life will inevitably be filled with challenges, but how we meet those challenges is up to each of us.

Failure Is Not an Option

It was a Saturday morning, and we were standing in our grocery store parking lot, our car doors and trunks open as one by one friends pulled up in their cars. We had scheduled two days for "socially distant and safe" drop-offs, and this year many decided to drop-ship directly to us. As was common in the COVID years, people's generosity was astounding.

We were delivering goodies as part of a holiday party and celebration for kids, meeting our sweet friend Sandra, aka Wonder Woman, at the Children's Village about an hour away. We had reached out to our network asking for items to help make Christmas special for the children. These were children living in foster care whose holiday, under the best of circumstances, is often spent overcoming hardship and disappointment. Now with COVID-19, the word *hardship* had taken on even more significance.

We drove in two cars, packed to the brim with snacks and the various requested clothing items, grateful that our crew of volunteers had come through as always, big time.

We pulled into the cul-de-sac as Sandra was just getting out of her truck with a trailer in tow. She wore a bright-red tank top and riding boots, her smile beaming from ear to ear. The children ran to her, eager for her to open the trailer.

"Merry Christmas, Miss Sandra!" they shouted.

"Merry Christmas to you," she bellowed, as if she were a tropical version of one of Santa's elves.

Sandra opened the slatted door trailer, led the ponies out one by one, and then handed the reins to each of the trained volunteer staff members standing in organized fashion next to her.

"I need someone to be especially watchful of Dolly," she said, looking at a little boy who was probably about eight or nine. "She's having a little bit of a tough day."

For Sandra, necessity truly was the mother of invention. Her youngest child, Jacob, was born with special needs. In researching his condition online, she stumbled on the website for Personal Ponies, an organization founded in 1986 that provides special ponies to therapeutic centers and individuals with programs that serve their communities. Sandra saw the magical impact the ponies had on Jacob, and she wanted to share this experience with other children in the community. Her involvement with the organization provided her with an outlet to help many people find happiness and connection. It became her passion.

"There is something real about animals and pets that relieves anxiety," Sandra said, a statement so many of us can agree with after sharing more time than ever with our pets during the pandemic. "People have tremendous needs, now more than ever," she said.

Once she realized the pandemic was not going to be a temporary situation, she gathered her cohort and adapted procedures to meet the community's needs. On every logistical level, it was daunting. But "failure is not an option," Sandra said, reminding us in the simplest and most profound way of how the power of love inspires hope.

Motivation and Meaning

Many of us are so grateful for the things in our lives that have given us a sense of purpose and helped us navigate what has felt like a somewhat helpless time. Elise talked to us about the importance of giving back and how it motivated her to write and publish a book. Her life is very reflective of the intergenerational overlaps and synergies we saw throughout the pandemic. A mother of five children ages twelve to twenty-two, she had a full house with all her kids home doing virtual schooling while she and her husband maintained their work together, providing coaching and leadership training to businesses and nonprofits. With three brothers and her parents nearby, she learned a lot about family relationships.

Her mother got COVID right at the beginning of the pandemic in March 2020. "It was an out-of-body experience," she said. "I called in the troops and used every contact I had to ensure that my mother would be okay." Thankfully, she emerged from the hospital healthy. Although it was a horribly scary time, Elise said she learned a lot from the experience.

"We're all a little bit stronger than we think we are," Elise said. "There aren't many opportunities that test our abilities like this one tested me." She said that although she knew it before, her mother getting sick reinforced in her the realization that you can never take anything for granted, and you must always be grateful.

Gratitude and giving are things that have always been in Elise's DNA. On the occasion of her fiftieth birthday, she decided to write a book because she wanted to help others. The book focuses on how to bring more positivity, gratitude, giving, balance, connection, calm, and success to life. Elise is very proud that her children got to witness this achievement.

"Our kids don't normally get to see what we do," she said. "During this time when all of us were together, they had a front row seat. They saw that I had a goal, and they bore witness from the beginning to the end," Elise said.

Clarity and Calm

Surprisingly, despite so much sadness and injustice in the world, the pandemic pause provided clarity for many people who had been lacking it in their lives for decades. For our friend Adrienne, this time was transformational.

"For me and for many others, this has been a time of huge awakening," Adrienne said. "It's been a time of transformation for those who wanted to transform."

In an unpredictable, uncontrollable time, we were forced to process our new reality. We had to stop and look within, evaluate our lives, and begin to navigate in new directions.

"For a while, there was a great deal of discussion on what our 'new normal' would be when we came out of this," Adrienne said. "As the pandemic dragged on, somehow people were forced to accept that we were actually already living our new normal each and every hour of each and every day. Surprisingly, people adapted."

Adrienne was able to shift from overdrive to pause and spend quality time with her husband, daughter, and new son-in-law. She was also inspired to become an advocate for causes that were important to her, making time to take an active role in the Parkinson's Foundation and the Women's Fund, an organization committed to gender equality, the advancement of women in the workplace, and equity and empowerment of women and girls. The slower pace gave many people the ability to be more present and aware of the blessings in their lives.

"Working to help others and be a voice for people who don't have the ability to advocate for themselves has meant everything to me right now," she said. "This time has been a reminder of the transformative power of love."

Millennial Mindset

Rachel, a friend and amazing Millennial in our community, told us that the pandemic pause was a journey to self-discovery. Years before when Rachel was living in Israel, she joined a women's circle called The Red Tent. It inspired her to go to graduate school to get her Master's degree in Educational Psychology as well as a Certificate in Reproductive and Maternal Well-Being. During the pandemic, she studied alternative medicine and acupuncture, laying the path for her career as a birth doula.

Throughout the pandemic, Rachel led meditation sessions virtually, creating community and holding space for people to come together when so many needed to practice mindfulness and reconnect with themselves. Rachel believes the most important things she has learned in life come from her personal growth, her parents, and the community she grew up in. She is intent on passing these lessons down to future generations as well.

Over and over in the time of COVID, we learned that in giving to others, we receive an immeasurable gift in return. The timeless words of Ralph Waldo Emerson tell the story. "To leave the world a bit better, whether by a healthy child, a garden patch or a redeemed social condition; to know that even one life has breathed easier because you lived. This is to have succeeded!" We couldn't agree more.

Lemonade

We have gained so much insight from our research and our year of honest and meaningful conversations. Here is a list of snippets of wisdom and lessons learned that we have gained to help us navigate life's bittersweet moments. Let's all keep learning, laughing, and living the lessons of the Lemonade Generation together.

Let's talk lemonade…

Lessons from Living with our Adult Children

○ Things don't always go as planned; adapt

○ Look for the good in everything

○ Learn to reframe your reality; our reality lives in our mind

○ Learn to let go

○ Embrace what you cannot control

○ Stay in your lane

○ Bite your tongue when necessary

○ Be grateful

○ Be hopeful, hope gives life

○ Choose faith over fear; keep the faith

○ Appreciate the ordinary, it becomes the extraordinary

○ Don't be the loudest voice in the room…listen and listen some more!

o Take care of our planet, live humbly

o Time is our greatest treasure, cherish it.

o Grow older with gratitude and grace

o Learn the stories of our grandparents and parents

o Listen to the wisdom and share the legacy of those who came before us

Lessons on Leadership and Creating Community

o Value the opinions of others

o Welcome diversity

o Stay open-minded

o Be a good listener

o Learn to compromise

o Be prepared, do your homework

o Be resourceful

o Be organized

o Have a vision, be bold

o Be a convener

o Be a consensus builder

o Respect people's time

o Respect rules

- Empower others; delegate
- Know when it's time to pass the torch with pride
- Check your ego…often
- Be the voice for those who have none
- Be welcoming and kind, always
- Be respectful
- Be a helper
- Show/share your passions
- Honor everyone's participation
- Make others feel appreciated and needed
- Live generously; we get what we give
- Make time to connect and really get to know people
- Do for those who cannot do for themselves
- Be a mentor
- Express gratitude
- There is no destination; life is the journey and growth is the accomplishment
- Have fun, laugh a lot
- Be the example for a beautiful future to follow

References

Preface

Surgeon General Dr. Murthy, Vivek Advisory, U.S. Department of
Health and Human Services, May 3, 2023
https://www.hhs.gov/about/news/2023/05/03/
new-surgeon-general-advisory-raises-alarm-about-devastating-
impact-epidemic-loneliness-isolation-united-states.html

Introduction

Fry, Richard, Passel, Jeffrey S. and Cohn, D'Vera, 2020, "A
majority of young adults in the U.S. live with their parents for the
first time since the Great Depression," September 4, 2020, Pew
Research Center
https://www.pewresearch.org/fact-tank/2020/09/04/a-majority-of-
young-adults-in-the-u-s-live-with-their-parents-for-the-first-time-
since-the-great-depression/

Butler, Katherine and Bannock, Caroline June 2, 2021
A sacrificed generation': psychological scars of Covid on young may
have lasting impact The Guardian
https://www.theguardian.com/world/2021/
jun/02/a-sacrificed-generation-psychological-scars-of-covid-on-
young-may-have-lasting-impact

Chapter 1: Generation to Generation

Gerhardt, Megan, Covid means Silent Generation is getting worst
of history, again. NBC News Nov. 29, 2020
https://www.nbcnews.com/think/opinion/covid-means-silent-
generation-getting-worst-history-again-they-deserve-ncna1248859

Chapter 2: Be the Air Dancer

Benedikt, Allison "17,000.000 Weeping Pregnant Women Can't Be Wrong, The mean-girl advice of What to Expect When You're Expecting, Slate, March 3, 2012
https://slate.com/culture/2012/03/the-mean-girl-advice-of-what-to-expect-when-youre-expecting.html

Jay, Meg, PhD, 2012, The Defining Decade, Twelve, Hachette Book Group, 2012, Introduction, Page XXX
(https://www.census.gov/content/dam/Census/library/visualizations/time-series/demo/families-and-households/ms-2.pdf)

Spock, Benjamin Baby and Child Care, 1946

Matheis, Liz PhD, 2020, "Parenting is Not About Controlling Your Child," Psychology Today, January 9, 2020
https://www.psychologytoday.com/us/blog/special-matters/202001/parenting-is-not-about-controlling-your-child

Chapter 3: Paralyzed in Our Sweatpants

Deloitte, Brandvoice, 2020, "The Importance of Mental Health Support in the Workplace" Forbes, August 4, 2020
https://www.forbes.com/sites/deloitte/2020/08/04/the-importance-of-mental-health-support-in-the-workplace/?sh=27b2184f3188

Horch, AJ Remote workers suffer from loneliness and isolationism as the pandemic in the U.S. drags on CNBC August 25, 2020
https://www.cnbc.com/2020/08/25/remote-workers-suffer-from-isolationism-as-pandemic-in-us-drags-on.html

Kugger, Jeffrey, 2021, "Domestic Violence Is a Pandemic Within the COVID19 Pandemic" Time, February 3, 2021
https://time.com/5928539/domestic-violence-covid-19/

Chapter 4: Release

Governor Whitmer, Gretchen, Executive Order 2020-43:
Temporary requirement to suspend activities that are not necessary
to sustain or protect life, April 9, 2020
https://www.michigan.gov/whitmer/news/
state-orders-and-directives/2020/04/09/executive-order-2020-42

The Deloitte Global Millennial and Gen Z Survey
https://www2.deloitte.com/global/en/pages/about-deloitte/articles/
millennialsurvey.html

Chapter 5: Sustenance for Survival

Silva, Christianna, 2020, "Food Insecurity in the U.S. by the
Numbers," NPR, September 27, 2020
https://www.npr.org/2020/09/27/912486921/
food-insecurity-in-the-u-s-by-the-numbers

"Baking Ingredients See Growing Demand During Covid-19
Pandemic," Businesswire, May 7, 2020
https://www.businesswire.com/news/home/20200507005587/en/
Baking-Ingredients-See-Growing-Demand-During-COVID-19-
Pandemic---ResearchAndMarkets.com

Aratini, Lauren, 2021, "Gardening Trend that Bloomed during the
Pandemic is Here to Stay" The Guardian, March 31, 2021
https://www.theguardian.com/lifeandstyle/2021/mar/31/
gardening-trend-pandemic-here-to-stay

Chapter 6: Hardship and Hope

Indiana University Bloomington Faculty Council Minutes, 1985
https://webapp1.dlib.indiana.edu/bfc/view?docId=B17-1986

Taylor, Alan, "Music and Encouragement From Balconies
Around the World," The Atlantic, March 24, 2020
https://www.theatlantic.com/photo/2020/03/
music-and-encouragement-from-balconies-around-world/608668/

Thoreson, Angela, 2021 "Helping people, changing lives: 3 health benefits of volunteering," Mayo Clinic Health Systems, September 16, 2021
https://www.mayoclinichealthsystem.org/
hometown-health/speaking-of-health/
helping-people-changing-lives-the-6-health-benefits-of

Viglucci, Andres, 2021, "Samoas cookie cocktail? Miami nonprofits get creative to raise money in the pandemic," Miami Herald, Updated February 5, 2021
https://www.miamiherald.com/news/local/community/miami-dade/article248991735.html

Philanthropy News Digest, March 29, 2020
https://philanthropynewsdigest.org/news/
jewish-federations-of-north-america-launches-covid-19-coalition

De Smet, Aaron and Pacthod, Daniel and Relyea, Charlotte and Sternfels, Bob, 2020, "Ready, set, go: Reinventing the organization for speed in the post-COVID-19 Era," McKinsey and Company, June 26, 2020
https://www.mckinsey.com/business-functions/organization/
our-insights/ready-set-go-reinventing-the-organization-for-speed-in-the-post-covid-19-era#

Executive Summary, McKinsey and Company, "How COVID-19 caused a global learning crisis," April 2022
https://www.mckinsey.com/industries/education/our-insights/
covid-19-and-education-the-lingering-effects-of-unfinished-learning

Levinson, Meira and Markovitz, Daniel,"The Biggest Disruption in the History of American Education, The Atlantic, June 23. 2022
https://www.theatlantic.com/ideas/archive/2022/06/
covid-learning-loss-remote-school/661360/

Temple Beth Am, Miami Florida
https://www.bethambasketball.com/
teams/?u=BETHAMBASKETBALL&s=basketball

Chapter 7: Loss and Loneliness

Pelley, Scott, "Stories from those who lost loved ones to COVID-19," CBS News, 60 Minutes, January 31, 2021
https://www.cbsnews.com/news/
covid-19-deaths-families-60-minutes-2021-01-31/

Walsh, Colleen, 2021, "Young Adults Hit Hardest During Pandemic," Harvard Gazette, February 21, 2021
https://news.harvard.edu/gazette/story/2021/02/young-adults-teens-loneliness-mental-health-coronavirus-covid-pandemic/

Chapter 8: Realigning Relationships

Rubin, Courtney, 2021, "Manage Your Divorce Expectations" The New York Times, January 30, 2021
https://www.nytimes.com/2021/01/30/at-home/manage-your-divorce-expectations.html

Leslie, Ian, 2020, "Why Your 'Weak Ties' Friendships May Mean More Than you Think" BBC, The Life Project, July 2, 2020
https://www.bbc.com/worklife/article/20200701-why-your-weak-tie-friendships-may-mean-more-than-you-think

Kennedy, Kelli, "COVID-19 pet boom has veterinarians backlogged, burned out," AP News, May 12, 2021
https://apnews.com/article/lifestyle-pets-coronavirus-pandemic-business-health-5047e430ce612609e8e21f557c60b900

Levy, Vicki, and Thayer, Collette, 2019, "The Positive Impact of Intergenerational Friendships," Washington, DC: AARP Research, May 2019; revised February 2020
https://doi.org/10.26419/res.00314.002

Davis, Michelle, "Despite Pandemic, percentage of older adults who want to age in place stays steady," AARP Research, November 18, 2021
https://www.aarp.org/home-family/your-home/info-2021/home-and-community-preferences-survey.html

Chapter 9: Faith Reimagined

Estrin, James, 2020, "Staying Apart, But Praying Together," The New York Times, November 15, 2020
https://www.nytimes.com/2020/11/15/nyregion/nyc-coronavirus-religious-worship.html

Chapter 11: The Great Outdoors

Sperling, Nicole, 2020, "When Tom Hanks, Hollywood's Everyman, Gets Coronavirus," The New York Times, March 12, 2020
https://www.nytimes.com/2020/03/12/business/media/tom-hanks-coronavirus.html

Ellis, Emma Grey, 2021, "The Lasting Impact of Covid-19 on Homelessness in the US," WIRED, January 28, 2021
https://www.wired.com/story/covid-19-homelessness-future/

Chapter 13: The Power of the Pause

Weir, Kristen, 2020, "Life after COVID-19: Making Space for Growth," American Psychological Association, Vol. 51, No.4, June 1, 2020
https://www.apa.org/monitor/2020/06/covid-life-after

Selig, Meg, "Getting Older? 14 Ways to Bounce Back from Aging Challenges," Psychology Today, September 4, 2019
https://www.psychologytoday.com/us/blog/changepower/201909/getting-older-14-ways-bounce-back-aging-challenges

Newport, Cal, 2021, The Joys of Approaching Life as an Amateur, The New York Times, January 12, 2021
https://www.nytimes.com/2021/01/12/books/review/tom-vanderbilt-beginners.html

Campbell, Leah, 2020, "How Lockdowns Have Helped Improve Some Mother-Daughter Relationships," Healthline, August 5, 2020
https://www.healthline.com/health-news/how-lockdowns-have-helped-improve-some-mother-daughter-relationships

Chapter 16: Passing the Torch

United States Census Bureau, 2018, "An Aging Nation: Projected Number of Children and Older Adults," US Census Bureau, March 13, 2018, Revised September 6,2018 and October 8, 2018
https://www.census.gov/library/visualizations/2018/comm/historic-first.html

Brooks, David, 2021, "What is Community Today, Big Question," Moment Magazine, July1, 2021
https://momentmag.com/community/

Acknowledgments

Good Work, Grit and Gratitude was our labor of love during a time of sadness and uncertainty in our world. We are so grateful for the wisdom, inspiration, and stories people shared, for their hopes, fears, funniest moments, and how their purpose evolved when the world was on pause. Thank you to all those who completed our survey, participated in our projects, and connected with us in the Zoom room, helping keep us sane when every day felt like Groundhog Day.

To Jennifer Browdy, a gifted writer, editor, publisher, and friend, we so appreciate the serendipitous way our paths crossed and that we are aligned in our mutual missions to right the world. Thank you for helping us "sit in our stuff" and distill the true meaning and message of our memoir.

Thank you to Laurie Friedman, Kimberly Standiford, Linda Hatton, Leah Messing, Susan Lafer, and Elizabeth Biondo for your expertise and encouragement in helping us bring this work to fruition.

Thank you to all those who serve their communities, bringing kindness, compassion, and advocacy at a time when it is so needed.

And thank you again to our families, our cast of characters in the Lemonade Generation, for continuing to be our teachers for life's most precious lessons.

About the Authors

Adrian Dubow and Laura Koffsky, two dear friends, have been active professionals and volunteers in the Greater Miami community for more than thirty years. They are passionately dedicated to making a difference in the lives of others. In 2014 they launched Good Work Miami, LLC, a resource for individuals, organizations, and philanthropists that emphasizes collaboration, leadership development, and connecting people to opportunities for advocacy, engagement, and purpose. Adrian and Laura have received many accolades for their expertise in mission clarity, communication, board development, and organizational succession. Laura is a graduate of Indiana University and the Wexner Heritage Foundation. She and her husband Dan have three adult children and one grandchild. Adrian, a graduate of the University of Arizona, is a certified life and happiness coach. She and her husband Ken have two adult children. Both Laura and Adrian are based in Miami. *Good Work, Grit and Gratitude* is their first book.

Find out more at Goodworkmiami.org.

A beautiful, uplifting memoir that explores family, love, personal growth, raising children and how our children raise us as well. *Good Work, Grit & Gratitude* is written by two accomplished women and close friends; by the time you finish this book, you will feel they are your friends and confidants as well.

—Rabbi Rachel Greengrass,
Temple Beth Am, Pinecrest Florida

Writing a book during a global pandemic—what better example of "making lemonade" can there be? Bravo, ladies!

—Susan Cortellessa, decorator and community
volunteer, Southport, Connecticut

The humor, honesty, and empathy that Adrian and Laura share make this book a source of inspiration and hope. We could all use the lessons they share about the importance of finding joy, gratitude, and purpose in life's most challenging moments.

—Elizabeth Biondo, executive editor, attorney
and community leader, Miami, Florida

This book, written with love, humor and optimism by good friends, is a wise evocation of the journey they took with their adult children during COVID.

—Julie Greiner Weiser, Board Chair, Goodwill South Florida

A heartfelt and therapeutic memoir of life seen through the lens of resilience, adaptation, and gratitude.

—Sheila Matz LCSW, adult, teen and family psychotherapist, San Francisco, California